ANATOMY OF KEYS

ANATOMY OF KEYS

STEVEN PRICE

Brick Books

Library and Archives Canada Cataloguing in Publication

Price, Steven, 1976-
    Anatomy of keys / Steven Price.

A poem.
ISBN-13: 978-1-894078-51-1
ISBN-10: 1-894078-51-9

  1. Houdini, Harry, 1874-1926—Poetry. I. Title.

PS8631.R524A53 2006   C811'.6   C2005-907694-1

We acknowledge the Canada Council for the Arts, the
Government of Canada through the Book Publishing Industry
Development Program (BPIDP), and the Ontario Arts Council
for their support of our publishing program.

The author photograph is by Esi Edugyan.

The cover design is by Kevin Price.

The book is set in Minion.

Design and layout by Alan Siu.

Printed and bound by Sunville Printco Inc.

Brick Books
431 Boler Road, Box 20081
London, Ontario N6K 4G6

www.brickbooks.ca

For my parents,
Bob and Peggy, with love

Contents

Hou'di-ni, 1. hu'di-ni; 2. hu'di-ni, Harry (4/6 1874 -   ) American mystericist, wizard and expert in extrication and self release, - hou'di-nize, vb. To release or extricate oneself from (confinement, bonds, or the like), as by wriggling out.

— *Funk & Wagnall's New Standard Dictionary*, 1920

escape. ME. also *eschape*, OF. *eschapper* (*échapper*), ONF. *escaper* (cf. It. *scappare*, Sp. *escapar*), from *ex* and *cappa*, cloak. To put off one's clothes, escape, the idea being that of leaving one's cloak in the clutch of the pursuer.

— Ernest Weekley, *Etymological Dictionary of Modern English*

❧

The natural crowd is the *open* crowd; there are no limits whatever to its growth; it does not recognize houses, doors or locks and those who shut themselves in are suspect.

— Elias Canetti

To have no other anger but public anger, this is to suffer exile.

— Victor Hugo

There is no excellent beauty without strangeness.

— W B Yeats

❧

In the domain of values, a key closes more often than it opens, whereas the doorknob opens more often than it closes. And the gesture of closing is always sharper, firmer and briefer than that of opening.

— Gaston Bachelard

❧

Whát I dó is me: for that I came.

— Gerard Manley Hopkins

In these memoirs or recollections there are gaps here and there, and sometimes they are also forgetful, because life is like that.

— Pablo Neruda

Now there are no bonds except the flesh.

— Gwendolyn MacEwen

Make it tight.

— Houdini

Of Origins
and Other Heirlooms

I

The trunk alone understands the journey.

Frail chest of my young mother, cage of rib
and shunted blood she held me to, rich smell
of garlic and oil, her rubbed warmth a salve
for my childish sleep. The frail chest our crossing
became, a rattling Atlantic steamer whose hull
held us all shut tight in filth and a heaving dark.
Frail chest my father is nailed in, coffin of rot
and poverty, the gnawing of worms loud
at his ears of that closing the grave must mean.
And grief, old death, the frail chest
a word can be.
                    For it is also the fist
hauling the strap of a scraped crate across a stage,
and it is the yellow arbutus and the cat's slow throat
and the milkish cry of boys at breakfast above a street
smoking off early frost. For it lurks in the shadows
of an unlit closet rustling with mothballs, dusty scarves,
it is the bed we are born to and the bed we are buried in,
cradle and coffin, and it is the five great books when shut
and the five great books when open, and it is, it is,
the glass eye in the box in the attic that watched us, a bend
in the bone, blood in the lung, grin in the fierce daguerreotype,
it is the closing and the opening as one. Old oak at the filthy glass,
I know your sadness, I've scraped that sill all my life to open
what is shut from me, lock or door or lid, my father's window
of earth, but I'll raise it now, a lid battered and green as a sea
where this life or the last is packed and bolted twice –
all stories are an opening and closing
of lids, dark trunks docked at a darker pier.
All things open here.

II

All August Greigh's Circus rattled and groaned
its carts closer, closer; garish clowns leered

their grim shrunken leers from posters furling brown
with sun in a storefront glass our ghostly mirrored

faces drifted from, to, and back to; dust draining
smokily off the lanes. Sunfat, itching, we'd flail

the hot weeds digging for coins, fish hooks, straining
for what ripple in the fields we could not say.

Closer, closer it came. Stakes, twine, old sheets: a tent
all our own was raised up, boneless, it wilted

to the left each time Ma's washline buzzed or bent
with shirts, that blessed wire we'd pinned a wall to.

I myself was the secret. Ehrich, Prince
of the Air, acrobat of backyard big tops,

a dangled blade of wind. Caped, in short pants
and red tights, a mulch-black jersey crinkled up

above my ribs, I'd hang head-first and blood-full
and grin gruesomely, the dry grass ruddering

in my fingers: its love for me was dreadful.
And Father's sigh; and Mother shuddering –

so we act and go on acting. As if we'd known
what it was we waited for, what we'd wanted, in that ground.

III

Not the austere unlit hall. Not the tenement
ceiling scraping its sad unlovely doors
above us shut. Not floorboards creaking and worn,
not that. And not us, in our hollow of cement.
But the listening. Reciting *Robert-Houdin.*
The nearness to it. Knowing in French an added *i*
meant *likeness.* Above us, Ma's *Theo! Ehrie!*
set my brother giggling: Ehrie Houdini –
and something shivered in me, strange
and tongued like a bell, an unseen door
unlocking above us. Our dark gaze gone upward:
a seething love in the given and not earned.
That austere unlit hall, set echoing again.

Ehrich. All my life the kilter and sag of it
like a mattress, *ehrr-ich,* its deep haul and drag
of coils wheezing, of Bess' wet gasp, *Ehr, Ehrie* –
and that unexpected *ich* like the click of a door.

Weiss in the iron vise of a keyshop; as in white,
as in the brilliant white breasts of Bessie Rahner;
and fist-stamped in *Houdini* a meaty, bruised *who.*
Hooded like a boxer's eye.

For there is no alone
in our lives. It was in Appleton
I think, in our shed's frame,
in its kerf and bulk of grain
where I'd hid in burlap bags
to wait Mother's fury out
or my own small fury out
when a voice hissed clear
and plain. Rats flicked, firked

from the sacks; a pail clanked
in the gloom; it came again.
A dark stirring seething
and glaring. Darkly it called me
by name.

IV

Stern as the finger of God. Fisted soft as felt.
The scent of his oiled grip still dank in its grain,
Father's cane crunked and heaved his laboured
stride of dust, turf, sod, dust, earthily insistent;
each step stabbed dirt, stirred him deeper in.

🌱

In the rusting candle light of his attic study
old Schtorr bent low, reeking of pork and garlic.
What mattered was the shape of lettering to wrist,
not speed of the line: all our lives are claimed
in the writing of our names. Precision. Density. Age.
I was so small he stacked cushions of books for me
to reach his oak veneer; I learned my name belonged
to the grasp of forefinger and fist, to a slanted shaft,
to the brace and heft of grip: not of mine, not to me.
Solemnly he'd rustle and blot, scratch a line, each page
knarred, ink-rubbed: in that candle's pitch and toss
he held loose the word that in holding held all else aloft.

🌱

Stick, staff, crutch, cane, cudgel, truncheon, switch,
her love slumped in harness, staggered lagged in it.
Her small fingers folding apelike as dusk ruddled
in her room, and us, two boys barrowed in our mother's
skirts, love a gust riffling bedclothes, ruffling curtains;
like black wool we unravelled, dark spools in her lap
amid the barbed click, tock, click of her knitting needles,
this clockwork of slender bones in yet more slender wrists,
this small stick, staff, crutch, cane, this cudgel, truncheon, switch.

🌱

Old exodus, old doubt of slaves.
I knew the story long before the language:
how in Egypt a scurled and snarling sand flayed

even the dour sun, God's hand an ever-drifting acreage
of heat. How cats unfurled like smoke in a courtyard,
past a stone Pharaoh glaring his casual feline glare,

on past a slave in rags. All exile is desert: God's hard
ideal of cleanliness is not enough to heal
a ravaged man of doubt; and Moses staggered scarred

by doubt. Shawls, voices, a creak and slap of well
water in a sour rusting pail. Aaron led him in
and sat. O I knew it well, brothers gifted with spells:

The rod Aaron casts shall fast become a serpent –
the day's hot wind-sift and word-sift railing on.
I too faced a god that freed Himself of all things,

I too became like the deep lightless desert: rent,
gashed open, a miracle of the ordinary fiery east:
daybreak: the white necessary void of page-end.

So. Sundrunk Cairo 1908. A street magician shrieks,
grasps it taut, rigid, that blue cobra flexing tight.
This, the miracle of Aaron's rod.
                              Then the release:
coil and curl, slither and sluggish wriggle into the light.

Bess loathed it, that glassed-in cabinet
of wands. Greyed ashwood, lathed and bleamed
a sullen deceitful softness, it squatted claw-footed

in our foyer, its panes splintering the late winter
light. She swore a coldness swirled round it.
Here Kellar's stout oaken twist hung; Frikell's slice
of birchwood; here the climbing contorted woody vine
Chung Ling Soo spun. The knap and knag of them.
Frail relics. Gutted and stuffed. A past laid claim to.
And I felt it, here, the old astonishment, that we do not lean
but support; how to explain to Bess what we bear?
Behind one worn staff, in a gloam and slow hush
of cabinet dust, Father's old cane kept.

Bess: I hear his burled and warm step yet.

V

This was in the long ago. Before oaths, us,
before the almost passed. A butcher's awning
in cold rain, the sleek cobblestones black, and her
fluid dipping figure dragging back the red door
and slipping past, slipping in. I watched her
among the blades, blocks, tiles scrubbed brutally clean,
the glass streaming; and since I had not failed her yet
I followed her in, drenched, my ruddied ears bare,
in where the hot drain and bloodbox of the heart
rasped hard, hooked naked as a braid of meat, hoisting
its glut and splay of brown paper to weigh creaking
and absolved: life, in the soft sawing of blood,
the wet ropes of blood.

VI

The last hand to hold my father held him here.
Machpelah Cemetery.
              Ma lurked, a soft box of skin,
as Bess shied graveside, solemn, that he might know her.
Hands hooked steady as a kedge and holding fast.

Or held fast. With its grizzled brick,
its clanking pipes and felt-and-dye stink,
that grim basement hat-shop became a kind of cabinet
she could step in and fasten close around her;
all gust-tangled hair, scrub-palmed, shabbily
she'd lurk there, a stranger to herself, drawn in
to bare the puck or play of fat-flowered brims
that hat by hat she yet might take the line of,
might drape and slant and tock and fidget
at a looking-glass until what looked back was not
what looked in but an apparition of the almost,
the unworn, of the anything-goes-and-to-come
drathing her last, too-lucid days of girlhood.

              Now I come to this
with her beside me, shining salt on her thighs,
crushed wet leaf between them, I come to this
with her: old, she will open like a book, dry or soft,
each fold a warm papery fug of ink; old, I will rest
my face like this, an ear pressed to her rib, listening.
For she is finer to me than a thousand thousand clocks,
more striking than sickled cuffs, this letter I write
is a sack unfilled, these lines without her air,
golden burlap, aridity. In August the streets rain,
she is the exact shade of a bruise or winter plum;
all autumn she is white as peeled bark; brilliant grains
of sand tack the boardwalk at her feet, a small sifting

of the earth. I come to this with her: I have loved
warmth, blackness, husks of sex, golden Beatrice,
Beatrice my Budapest.

The jellied give of locks, greased in,
shuddering, the tightening of pins
sliding home: all of it fingered,

lubricious, enterable and entered   .
into like language. Salt-thick. A loose
vaginal groove of pick and key.

How she'd stub or shamble into trunks,
ladders, chests, awkward before a crowd
yet glide with the careful verity of monks
when alone, when her wasp-slender waist flowed
with the relied-upon and regular-as-rust
assurance some goodness must come next.
Or her hard-knuckled washtub hands at dusk
flexing that stiff grace all hurt flesh collects,
a sort of bruised largesse which steadied her words
like one long jeered at. I loved her for such things.
And her unsullied generous laugh that cured
street-grime, stall-grit, the awful grag of things.
Thin and thrush-eyed and strange.
Listing awkward with life, as with a bad leg.

Bess naked naked naked. Shy and lightly dimpled.
Her thighs freckled like long-moist leather
held in their golden hairs astonishment
and the furred inelegant calligraphies

of the ordinary. Mud-filled ruts in streets;
soft shrouds rotted like sailcloth; the woodbent,
rent, forty-seven nails of my father's sleep –
O I admit a seam-split, bulging, abundant love,
a drawn-up, drenched-off, brimful, dripping-with-it love
that sated all and overspilled our sleep;
I admit to sodden joy, laughter, and our odd
lack of wonder, as if it were enough to live
blessed in it, blind;
                    one does not ask who gives.
Holy holy holy. Even the seraphim cover their faces from God.

And all at once all burst in ripeness and in light –
          pressed close, luminous, I did not know
and knew, this must, her, Beatrice, blazed hurt
          and heartening, be wayfarer, be water in this life.

VII

Such newsreels flicker still. His mother in a crowd
shawled soot-dark and frail. The roped-off ledge
of a dour steel bridge; ten thousand blazing throats and the stretch

of girders toward a stinking canal. His chained ankles
flickering; then his shrug to her, shy, as if rising
dully from some couch or half-eaten lunch to step but a moment out

when he plunges. The wet thump of flashbulbs flaring the river,
rail, sunlight, his grey flesh gone in that lazy wash of foam;
crowds jostling in, hushed; a shadow ripples the water –

   but true suffering is an art like any art; it must be learned.
   In a peeling kitchen in Appleton a child's knees grind
   the lip of a tub, his knuckle crooks the shy hairless fish
   of his sex,

   he grins *Ma look at this!*, scrunches his nose: is gone.
   Heels farting the washtub walls. Hair strangling the oily surface.
   She hears it still: her old chair rasping back, that flat skitter

   of peeler and skin and potato meat across the floor,
   in her ears the fast plaited river of Budapest, of girlhood
   and quick as a gasp she is up, crying *Nein, nein Ehrich* –

his nose blowing careful air and him pausing
beneath the gurgling pockets of breath just long enough
to draw out the awe in her dark face.

VIII

Then guy-ropes creaked, plashed, and I sank
to a muscular thud of blood. That cage of water
windowing darkly round me. Ankles bound.
My slow hair untangling. I sighed and a crowd sighed;
fear in the stagelamps, fear clicking at the glass:
nothing felt farther from Appleton, nothing nearer.
Ma's strained love I'd dragged down like a lock,
dragged until no longer strange to me,
its spill of thick soil, its black shawls
of Budapest, of her life before mine;
I lived in her love as if of its element,
swallowed her ribs, ate the thin dream
of a son's first escape: his twisting
shyly in her frozen kitchen,
hissing *Shake me Ma I'm magic*,
darkness shining from her black eyes
set like lanterns of unlighted oil, and her
knuckles, her knuckles, taloned
fiercely in his flesh, and her shaking
shaking him, the cupboards seething
dark with faces, slitted eyes, the shrill
clashing of her silverware –
and then her laugh, clean like a blade,
as the year's bright coins spilled forth from his hair.

IX

We sat still, our lantern-tallow houring down
the hours. Father, fist-bolstered, brooded grim
at our dark table as Ma bashed a kettle, frowned

in her sink at the scruffled beard he had become.
Her ragged apron wet. And his white womanly hands
luminous with an unworldly light, fumbling some

on the whorled oak before falling still again;
he hardly breathed, hardly breathed, hardly breathed.
It seemed the hiss of cloth fustled round him

even then, that brutal must and sift of chalk
on bolts of wool he would end his days by mending.
He sighed; the drapes wrestled a creeping dark –

when, in, it burst, that thing; all flack and wing
and furied battering of sink, dishrag,
kettle, sink, and off, up, a fierce thing hurtling

high in that kitchen its harsh batlike stagger.
From what had it come? Drawn by what light?
A black clatter in the crockery, a thing all drag

and beak and featherless slap raftering from eye
to slow eye. Father funnelled a cone of papers;
it dipped and cut past and he struck hard out,

forceful, as if brute will could bring back order
to the twisting room, he lunged, struck, struck – but missed.
And all at once it lit past like a long blurred

cloth for the half-shut glass, the curtained kitchen glass.
Broke against it skullfirst. The window warbled shock.
That thing struggled, flopped about the sill, hissed;

then scissored in grim precision out to the black
world. And left him gasping, his pale fists
at his thighs. His wife's eyes glinting in the dark.

X

All autumn I lay between them, tangled in their cot
like a stiff shrunken limb, a pale child grown paler
in a room bristling with burnt spice, oils, muslin.
Our sheets stank of sickness, wilted around us.
I prayed greedily: too young to lose a father.
All autumn I lay *between* them, his voice the absence
of voice, his throat the absence of throat; a man less
flesh than bedclothes, whiskers, teeth. Ma stoked
coals we could not spare. In a cabinet his books
curled their dreadful damp hands as if in sleep, a fug
of paper hazing all of us. I lay still. A kind of line
between the death of my father, the life of my father.
Still he shrank beside us, in what little light he'd left us.
His dark coals luffing and fading like lungs.

XI

Father I begin here.
At Theo's gasp, at Mother's grip,
his squat legs lunging behind her
as we surged home on Twelfth: slip
of scraggled children, shroud of widow's shawl.
Our tenement, black above cart-racket, hoof-clips,
stall-cries; I slowed: and like that, you hauled
the sackcloth off. This world, roaring bright and harsh and rare.

Cancer of the tongue. Rot
of clotted words. Weekly, air
wore at your throat, bloated it, jawed
and bruised and bled it. Prayer
hurt worst, German a language of blood
and molar, of bitter verbs, rancid, spare.
I washed your lips; do men of God
suffer more or less? I washed your lips.
Suffer not.

Like sweat, like broiled meat
you thickened to a smoke-rank stink
as the months passed; your oilish heat
hung cellar-dank in our sink
and bedsheets, a bookish stench, a brackish stench.
Death I learned is odor: Mother, in a blink
of sadness at the bath, soap-sweet, steam-drenched,
while all I smelled was sweat; while all I smelled was meat.

Mute then as glass
or rain, mute now as mildew
or ash: how blunt and awful a task
childhood became. You:
a brooding thrummed silence; blood in my blood.
I listened for you then, Father, as I listen for you now:
this bellowing bursting grief, this thud
of lung-thick loss was suddenly only hush, was suddenly rustle and rasp.

Theo hissed: *Touch him.*
Bedthick, unbundled, your body a glaze
laid dry, lamp-brown, thin,
murkish and wrong. Amazed
at what I'd done, I fingered the shroud, fingered the sheet –
touch him, and I did, I do, I reach out, still raise
your palm's cold slab: all bone, all meat.
Hour by hour this horror is the hand I hold you in.

XII

You hunch bedside, a slim child afraid of eyelids and dusk.
      A battered door bangs shut. He lies
scrunched like a fist; blue drapes shut fanglike at the sill.
      A stink of bad teeth. Of tongues
made meat of. *Ehrie*, it comes: *There is no life but the life*
      we are given. God is a sliver of teeth,
a devouring. Fear him. And the illness a life must lead to,
      the draped line of a woman's hips
wide with loss, He is these also, *yes*, the muffled scrack of rats
      in the walls, all a boy knows of death, *this*
also is God. The curtains slice in that light.
                        Not wind: a breath.

XIII

... except it was Thursday, listen: all week with her window
nailed shut in a drench and crunch of ice, he stood in his death
outside its sill, a slow wisp, patient as glass, while Cecilia
darkened within: alone like a bruise. He stood; she slept
unseeing, sunlight ripening round him and her and runnelling teeth
of icemelt downpane; it was beautiful, a streaming light Cecilia
yet could not wake to, a fluid glare he had missed while alive...
... except it was Thursday, he'd been dead all week; a long white
veil lifted at that tenement sill and again fell; *listen*: she lay
alone like a bruise and he watched her wake, nowhere to go,
he stood in his death and he waited, thinking *Balabosta, you
too stand here, alone: nothing between us but air.* She curled
as if in a draft, untangled a sore white ankle as if to rise, go to
him, a mad nightgowned walker weeping furied and shaken:
Weiss, Weiss, you left me your children; what have you done?

The Escapologist

ncerning escapes – Keys and ropes and the tools of a life – Learning the geek effects –
The ballad of Houdini – The Metamorphoses trunk – A dangling man – Proverbs
of escape – Concerning his enigma – England – Imitators and other wretches –
Voyages – Flight – To Russia – Hauntings – Concerning what he was, what he is

XIV

Key: Ehrich.
            Houdini.
                   He knew himself wholly
in that other. Ropetrod or strangled stage
right, rumpled in trunk tricks, flushed, tousled,
allowing magic's antic, contrary, quarrelsome
right to brag and strut and bolster men
awake to strangeness and the bloodclock in
their skulls. Coalbox. Bolt-Ladder. Paper Crate.
Weed-Tire Chain-Grip. Each weird escape a kind
of anger felt at being held hard down
as if such letting-go or slackening
might drain him of his self: the struggle less
a slaking of the fists than of the mind.
His life raised and raised again as metaphor;
his words laid out the tackled thunk and buckle
of chests, of leather-wrought thickened holdings hoarding
thicker words like coins: never less himself
than in the language of old locks, closings,
the given. Life a kind of end-stopped line,
measured in the breath and bloodbeat of it;
he turned from all of that. Escapes each night
stank of musty centuries of magic:
the stiff, leathern satchel his flesh became.

Latch: He held his life in his teeth like a key.
Freedom meant restraint, finding one's place:
a warm rope fed and bellied him at the first,
a cold rope will lower his casket at the last.

XV

        The stories keys could tell,
still, of the rusted throats of cells, skeletal keys,
and keys knuckled like fingers, keys harsh-voiced
and stunned like a blaze of cold bells, copper keys,
birch keys, keys reeking of mulch and wet moss,
more, the excellent French names of keys, all eager
thigh, fluid, stamen, fumbling at locks themselves,
the tongue another muscular key at his lips, slipping
free, for he was careless, Bess, careless with such keys,
keys to trunks, chests, desks, keys choked in his gut
or wedged under nails, fang-toothed keys, and keys
drowned in jars like small dark snails, consider
the stubborn silences of these, what stories
they could tell; Bess, even this band on his finger
shines, a key.

XVI

        Rope:
  sleek sashcord, escapologist's skin,
          umbilical of the drowned, shrouded hood
hanged men bladder and drag and stretch out in;
wildfire ripple of rumour through a crowd;
sheath, frayed bloodline, sinew of fire and flint,
          asleep in one's lap like a child or a cat
and like a child all ululation, all wailed lament;
rope of muscle, rope of bone, the elbow of it
          ever unbending; black intestine or spleen:
          dark many-cornered flesh a knot can be.
A kind of thread and weft he worked behind,
what bound him and unbound him, God to man:
Holy of Holies, spell, sky, prayer, wrist:
          the shaking of his father's hands in his.

XVII

Dusk. A stubbed candle flared, rent deep
the dark knots in her tent; she dragged it near.
Her eye sockets like blazing cuffs of bone
held an inner darkness. *These are the geek effects –*
the way light tattoos the chest, inks its skin;
the way a needle glides in epidermal and blind
as if stitching its long rasping thread to the lung;
the way a thumb scrapes blood to the tongue.
Stripped to the waist, nippled in blood, he sat
still, more still, her needle hooking a shame
his father had felt, eyes turned from the world.
She fixed the first cold brass buttons in his flesh.
Be still. Learn this. And the sky loosed a sorrow
the air had carried for miles, and a slow rain
flecked and tapped the tarp walls. A puddle
of grey wax cooled into a skin on her desk –
glinting buttons in a dish of light, spool of thread
moving end to end, nothing between them but flame,
a stink of sweat, candle-smoke, the darker things
filling that tent. Did he dream her fingers, soft,
twisting his topmost button, sliding it through its eye?
Something dragged at his shoulders, hauled the skin
into a wet heap on the floor: Houdini he was not;
just a boy stitched of darkness from a sky outside.
It was no great trick at all.

XVIII .i

To straddle the chair such that slack
is drawn, an elbow or knee of rope
wrinkling shin, throat, hipbone, chairback;

then to thrash, tip over, beat the air
like a boy beset by bees in the pines
of Appleton, as if a sting and flare

of swarming thorns unwound between
black trees, a fierce dark rigging
he'd flailed down. Like sunlight, not seen

but sharply felt. Yet now, to feel
less and less sure that anything
of ropes in all of that was real;

the savagery of bees descends like truth:
he'd been set upon by a kind of song
which linked the many rooms of this earth

by finding such sweetness in each one.

(Seated Rope Escape, Boston, January 1906)

XVIII .ii

That riveted iron boiler clanked
      and gurgled dully there
while hoses gushed and sluiced the tank
      until it held no air.
A bucket clanged. Houdini rose,
      brandishing an axe:
it was not true he would come to rue
      that night in Halifax.

Three stagelamps smoked and guttered lean,
      two fanglike lid-bolts grinned;
he struck and banged the boiler's seams
      for leakage near the hinge.
The rivets whitened knucklelike
      as liquid sucked them shut;
but it was not he they'd come to see.
      That crowd had come for blood.

Houdini lunked and scaled the tank,
      muscular and grim.
He gripped its rim by knee and shank,
      then let the crowd grip him.
A man can only hold his breath
      so long, he shouted down;
but it is not right you've come tonight
      half-hoping I might drown,

risking nothing more your own
      than nickels, or a laugh.
Hold your breath while I am down.
      See how long you last.
Casket-like that boiler loomed,
      its rippling waters black,
but it was no grave he'd come to brave
      that night in Halifax.

Houdini's stagehands loosed a line
   and took the axe from him;
he slithered in and floated blind
   as though within a womb
and watched the widened eye of light
   above him eyelid shut;
it was not air he latched out there.
   He latched out all he was.

That eerie belly held him warm,
   it shivered at each sound;
his blood beat like a bat up-barn,
   frantic, bashing round.
A spangled stagelight filtered in
   and lit his grey skin weak;
but he felt no fright as the locks shut tight:
   that lid was forged to leak.

At thirty seconds ladies gagged,
   at fifty-five most men;
one minute twenty an athlete sagged;
   the clock went round again.
Three swimmers choked, two divers next,
   but still that boiler sat;
at last one said, *He, he must be dead,*
   a man all thumbs and hat.

Three minutes ten. Four twenty-eight.
   No man can live so long.
A stagehand stood hefting his blade,
   the audience a throng
of throats and groans and fist-clenched thighs;
   death had seized them here;
for it's not in ease most men believe:
   true art is found in fear.

The axeblade glittered, menacing
      a bright ferocious grin,
suspended in its heft and swing
      it dragged the crowd's rage in;
yet there it hung, it hefted, hung,
      hung poised and trembled deep;
it was just this they'd feared to miss –
      when out he stepped. Free.

The curtains shook. Fine plaster fell.
      The audience had made it,
yet in that rush all somehow felt
      flushed, exhilarated,
and unaccountably depressed.
      Onstage the clock still stood.
For it was not he they'd come to see;
      that crowd had come for blood.

(Water Torture Cell Escape, New York, May 1907)

XIX .i

Love too felt locked
at times like a trunk
drag-chained yet not
to be escaped from.

Its lids banged
and creaked, a flash
of keys onstage.
A mouth shut fast.

For in all of this
a kind of changing
tethered him, left her
uneasy, estranged.

She'd tie his wrists
in sackcloth, tug
and lash each fist.
The burlap sagged.

Their trunk lid gaped.
A stuttered clunk
of chains, of ropes,
of spoon-dark locks.

Then blackness rose
shackling Houdini;
blacker lids closed;
the Metamorphoses –

That trunk, scraped
quick into a cabinet.
Bess, screeling drapes
shut all around it.

The crowd grown dense,
bellowing, *Two, three –*

and all at once
instead of her leaned

he, Houdini, all
muscle and stillness,
a cat on a sill,
the stunned applause

surging up, drapes
wheeled to the wings;
unknuckling the ropes
and knotted strings

of locks he hauled
back the lid to pick
from a writhing sack
the sack-lunked head

of his wife, dazed
as he'd been dazed,
as if by the joys
of an easy goodness.

(Metamorphoses Trunk Escape, Kansas City, April 1899)

XIX .ii

Observe the dangling man.
A dark cocoon of teeth.
In the tall air he spins
blood-fat, holstered
in his straitjacket, spins
heel-snagged then sags
bonelessly akimbo like gut-slit game
while boiled leather straps pinion
his wrists, a big gust tolls him hard;
observe him: what is horror to his fixed eye?
The earth a black blood-filled skull far below
where pocket watches flare with sun,
where streetcars brake as darker buildings loom
over swarms of drudging men. He writhes.
You raise a hand to your eyes to see.

(Aerial Straightjacket Release, Minneapolis, September 1915)

XX

from Proverbs of Escape

The torn rope is twice useful.
A chained wise man remains free. A chained fool escapes.
In old age even the butter-lid grins.
Lies of the illusionist. Truths of the illusion.
Thicker the cord, weaker the knot.
The tied trunk never tells the rope what it holds.
Where conscience is the door, privilege is the hinge.
When he is bound, the crowd is. When he is free, the crowd is not.
The fettered man's curses open only his own mouth.
In the Garden the key is no place. In Hell the key is every place.
Satan goes hidden. God goes unnoticed.
Shackled at daybreak, shadows. Shackled at dusk, lanterns.
No release without first being bound.
Skinniest wrists, hungriest cuffs.
Locks laugh not, weep not; but embrace all things with ease.
Knowledge into goodness. Wisdom out of goodness.
The new pick bends, the old pick breaks.
Mourning unties no knot. Praying unclasps no cuff.
He who conceals everything conceals nothing.
Never how it was done. Always how it was not.
Compassion. Attention. Praise. An anatomy of keys.
To leave the self is love.

XXI

Key: Openings terrify.

Flesh: Offstage, he looked
too ordinary in his strength to be so;
short and stumpish like a pugilist, he lived
by his fists, all ox-neck and thick root,
all barrel-chest, battered like a kitchen chair.
A man of collars, ties, lustrous black suits,
he'd wear his shirtcuffs rolled, lapels rumpled,
trousers badly creased until Bess fairly wept
to see him out the door; and in altercations
in the street he'd flare his scarred red hands
like scarves or terrible flowers; or pause,
stare, frown as if surprised to find a dime
in his pocket; or else peer off muttering,
thin-lipped, squint-eyed, his curled hair carved
down a vicious white line of scalp, forehead
naked and large as a hand, and like a hand
always opening –

Key: Only his eyes were still.
Fixed and fixed upon. Sleepless. Grey. Still.
And he seemed a very embarrassable man
for all that, wearied, haunted, as if whatever
he did he'd demand it bring a goodness
to the world, as if the opposite of good
were not evil but indifference. Being
in the world can also become habit;
he lived as if a knowledge not his own
lay visited upon him.

Flesh: And in the middle of it all
his blue cloth cabinet billowed secrets.
Escape became a kind of consolation
as it always was and is: he'd slip confined
behind his curtain and step suddenly free –
thickset, at ease, *free* – dangling from a fist

the loosed, smug, still-locked cuffs
or tear aside the drapery to show
a box or trunk still nailed casket-tight.
Nothing altered, yet all somehow changed;
as if to prove what binds men also unbinds.
He led by example. He reassured the age.

Key: Yet liberated nothing but himself;
and which self? Aping the belted frothing
man in all men, that blunt too-familiar
surge of blood, he'd writhe clear of cabinets
that all might see unleashed a madness in
the world. Straitjackets, strap-beds, crazy-belts,
buckled chairs: the appetites of men
horrified. To want to see such acts, to seek
reassurance in rituals like that:
what did his sufferings tell him of them?
Each night he'd work contorted, bleeding
in full view, knees lashing a littered stage,
clothes in shreds.

Flesh: But methodical. Clearly sane.
Men loved his gruff proprietary love.
Striding onstage like a boxer, arms flung wide,
he'd shout, *I'm Harry Houdini and I can beat
any man in the house.* He became in time
a hard burnished mirror held before a world
which failed to recognize itself.

Key: Mirrors, too, are openings.

XXII .i

He feared his own face everywhere.
Ghosting up out of the shine in things.
Out of the linen-shelf looking-glass, leering;
or dark stage-mirrors, their any-angled reflections
splattering light; in the murky fragged mirrors
spirits spoke to, strode through. He trusted none.
But prowled past their frames all fist and thighs
as if along the ribs of a stubborn cage;
as if boundless; as if the sullen hooded shades
he feared lurking there might fear him back.
For mirrors distorted discipline. Bent men
sideways. Shivered visions into being.
A light oozed from all things, hotel glass, spoons,
shopfront windows, dark asphalt after rain,
the silver hourglass slice of a lady's eye;
and nightly the bathtub's still water
stared up, rippling, nightly he stirred it
and it stirred, darkening
his hand as his hand
slipped in under –
          Thus the eye offends
itself. A figure kneeling in a closet mirror,
battered by the briny autumn light, its wrists
blazing like his own wrists in their dark chains,
its fingers stubbing too the slender nostril
of a lock he has struggled and struggled to learn.
His glare fixed upon the white wrists in the mirror,
upon, O, a shine twisting like the iridescent scales
of a sea, like the fire and flare of a key
glinting in stagelamps, listen, the true mirrors

are not mirrors at all, they hold us too
in their terrible iris of light.

They are the skins of still ponds nailed to our walls.

The framed shudder and gust of winter air.

What fear most resembles.

Us.

XXII .ii

Elegies. The north Atlantic waters creaked
their icy swells in the grey forever that is grief.
And in Paris oaks like amber streetlamps blazed
in a dusk he strolled by leaf-shine. But the haze
of snow in the carved-stone arches of Glasgow.
Or Spain, its tangled orchards of grapes gold
with late heat, the sun-glarred murmur of bees.
And the blue steam-tempered knives of Araby.
Voyages and returns. He seemed ever
to be leaving his life, ticket punched, never
to be arriving. Eyeing his mother dockside
while streamers drifted sadly to the wharf,
moorings splashing, the steamer's organ horn
set mournfully for sea. Her waving up fierce,
as if knowing. As if sighting a ship
beyond the ship, a darker crossing ahead.
Her rings glinting like a fistful of knives
in that light. Flaring. Then
vanishing.

XXIII .i

Yarra River, Melbourne, 1910

A reptilian shine in its waters. Black
as a chain, the Yarra glistered its hot muck
below the bridge. His legs frogged, ankles cuffed,
he peered flinchingly down for the fluid wake
of sharkfins;
        and leapt. Struck a stunned burst of silt.
Sank fast into pale weeds. In his toes a thing soft
as mud gave and gave but he flailed it off,
punched frothing upward, cuffs brandished in his fists,
his feet tangling yet that grey kicked-up stew –
A girl's corpse. A soupy staring mass.
              And his shin
thrashed in, in again, a horror he would live
and relive, all of it coming apart inside him;
his watchers wading hard, plunging bodily off
the bridge. Seeking not escape but a way in.

XXIII .ii

Diggers Rest, Australia, 1910

Sun-drenched, a scorching gale; still Diggers Rest
delighted, all fiery weed and fierce white sand
and his Voisin's crackling canvas wings in flight.

Ehrich loathed Australia. Gull-wristed, lost
in grimy blackened coveralls, he'd kick the land
clear of buried rocks, stumps, snags; or light

a rumpled cigarette, sigh, then scrub sunlight
into valves, struts, unpacked plugs. Diggers Rest,
not Melbourne: a tarp sealing his landed

plane. He slept badly, huddled in chill sand
under cold deliberate skies; and, worn in, lost
in that oldest form of escape, dreamed of flight.

Ashore at Port Said. The sad loping flight
of blue-necked cranes above the harbour lights,
heat rising from the sun-bleached walls, then lost –
Bess felt it. Long weeks still till Diggers Rest.

Harsh bells. Stalls. Camels bawled, stinking, in sand.
Her sandals crunched like links of chain in a land
silting all things, parasols, crowds, crates, a land
of hide-cured street fakirs straining after flight,

ropes, levitations, basket magic. White sand
seeping out loose sleeves in such clumsy sleight-
of-hand she laughed aloud. Not Diggers Rest,
flight, or dread; she felt delight only in what was lost.

Then whiteness. The lightness of his loss.
Fanged winds. Creak of buckling struts as grassland
kiltered, all hill and held breath at Diggers Rest.

Cold slap of tail canvas. Australia's first flight
in a thing heavier than air; he'd learned in light
of the modern age, a man of the ampersand,

of radio & reel. Stiff with hailed sand,
the engine glugged, roared behind; all fear lost
in that strange trembling skeleton of sticks, light,

cloth, piano wire. Spidery aloft, on land
it seemed a lumbrous kind of magic, flight.
A hard, bright thing in the skies of Diggers Rest.

XXIII .iii

Diggers Rest, Australia, 1910

Such faith alone felt heavier than air –
all of it pitched, winged, in a pollen sun
as the Voisin's struts vanished in glare.

Bleared goggles golden and dust-blown.

All fuel-box or heat, stalled in a sky dazed
as if from the blundering frenzied blades.

Then it struck, hard, a muscled air of flight
as he blustered on, a wind like river water
lifting him toward an astonishing light.

All darkness far below him in the earth.

Borne aloft on miracle, dazzle, the shining
not within all things but beyond all things.

Oil-fumes seared his face, as if reeling close
to cloud a gliding imperishable redness beyond
the dunes, that purity of light-drenched gusts.

His iris the one darkness. A last looking-on.

And if only an inner brilliance were blessed
in elevating man to God? He'd confess

to blood buoyant with light, violent
and quaking in an acre of immensities
no less strange for being ever overhead.

XXIV

Moscow, 1903

His dark arched carriage creaks across this page
and halts. An ice-cobbled hotel glints like steel
drenched in light; his arrival *became* the voyage:
a dream of ship-ribbed horses, fog, an unreal
surge of domed rooftops. Only fear felt real;
it slept in cold sheets, infected his hands –
ask any traveller: home is the harsher exile.
He slid a coin in the porter's pale hand
and his door clicked noiselessly shut, the black journey began.

Day and night he lived on blood-dark coffee
in that land, on corn soups ladled from cauldrons,
iced plums, on dried figs laid in tissue leaves
like the blue wrinkled thumbs of children.
And at all hours, in the walls, the cries of men.
Soft feet ghosting the halls. Slurred fiddle-tunes
creaking through his floor, in ceiling vents
a reek of cigars, a rasp of bolts being drawn:
man seemed but a thing dreamed up in rags at dawn.

For at dusk down winding alleys white faces
flared sullenly from sullen shopfront windows,
their ruddied ears wind-bloodied in that place
as if ashamed of it. His thick heart slowed;
he waded grieved and strange and a grey snow
blurred his bootprints in the cold; then a blown shape
staggered past, all at once of the long ago –
his frail father snorting wetly as flakes
stung his lips. He trudged grimly on. Tired of escapes.

A bed. Sprawled drapes. Tangled in the drapes, light.
A window's shine at the eye's edge like glarred ice
roused him blanket-bound, blinking raw at a street
of lurching convicts clashing past. His eyes
blurring, swollen, as in a dream: blood-dried

black bootprints, black scalps of men caked and shorn,
black carts lashed fast, creaking east. Dull grunts. Flies.
That black fist all men feared: a knock on his door
battering fierce like broken cuffs on a stage floor

the grey crowds seethed smokily to see. His flailing
in a crush of roped chairs. In low balconies
men jeering, a dark shine of polished railings,
clink of cut glass – then the soft gloved wheeze
of applause. His torn wrists sticky in shirtsleeves.
He lived on blood-dark coffee and in his drapes
light strangled and he strode his rooms glaring east,
that strong grim breaker of chains, trunks, chests, crates –
who could not escape the strict stanzas of his days.

Then the rumours in April proved real.
Real the slaughtered ruck of meat, teeth, hair, bone.
Real the rake and real the scythe and real
the rubbled blood-holy bricks of a pogrom.
In a drafty bookshop he withdrew a cold tome
and smelled spiced pastries, stew, and turning peered at
an old Jewess huddled at a lit stove, alone,
heard a bright shriek of children in the garret –
and all at once stood trembling. His flesh too full to bear it.

A snort of horses, scrape of ice-spoked carts
on flagstones: such ordinary sounds amazed
him. Pulp of God's sorrow, rind of God's heart.
His last day dawned dull and raw in a cold haze
his carriage sludged through, clattered out of, dazed
by the grey light. A herd of Jewish convicts lined
up clinking in the scaffold-dark marketplace;
he stared out, the ticket rumpled in his hand;
the true Sakhalin built its prisons in the mind.

Where a rickety wood synagogue once stood
a son dreams still his father's fevered dreams
and grips in his hand the hand of his God;
grief is a sickness in the bones: it consumes.
And jostled in that station he smeared his palms
down a beaded window, sighed wetly in
the ripe unwashed air, the jangled cries, fumes;
then waded that platform knee-deep in men.
Death flashed its darker finer passport; ushered him in;

and he sat eyeing the black stuttering tracks
soon wending faster past his railcar, a sky
all at once behind him. His pale face slack
in the blurred pane he peered past, as if to deny
the frail grey eye glaring fearful from his eye,
his hands white at his knees in the blinding
late shine. We face brutal unforgivable lives,
all of us. In the glass a red sun was bending
beyond the hills, its light fading. The day was ending.

XXV .i

What hadn't he imagined, or dreamed, or lamented?

Did he walk slumped among the stones of this world
to find at the last the longest road not his?

Faith: to be made wide by it, to be
next year in Jerusalem, to kneel at Machpelah:
is it sweet to suffer for what is right?

Did he believe in the touched or no?

Hoofkicked bloodily back, her left elbow
still fanked up in cartspokes like a braid of grass,
dark men gathering hatless, hushed, as she dangled
black-haired and boneless in the street's gutter;
or Ehrich drathing his father's corpse, a thing
thick-throated and foul, dank floorboards slumping
under it in the soft light while grey rabbis
shuffled past. Thus are we drawn to and led from
the mystery. Grotesque at his father's side,
bent in grief, he shut his eyes and saw her, that girl,
he felt his father's arm firm in his own, heard again
the crowd's murmur, a clatter of carts up the street,
his father's wet reluctant laugh in a fist: *Och, Ehrich,*
I mend men's cloaks now. Only God can mend
what you ask. His stooping on past. And then*:*
Come. They do not gather for her.

Then it was not. Iron bedframe, sheets, stained walls spared
the belligerence of grief, Ehrich did not seal the eyes, did not

drag a shroud at its jaw, no sleeve or stitched hem gaped wide,
rent in his fists, water left unspilled at the threshold, it was not,

not lips blistered like a skin of soup, not bloated lids,
not the gnarled foot on the mattress, its heels did not

face a widened door, this, a gesture which is no longer,
a son stubbing a white candle at a pillow, crying, it was not

the tallow, wick, wax of it, he had loved. On the bureau a mirror,
in the mirror a shining window; all at once an iridescent waterglass

gathers in its light. Austere
                              and cold. Wholly without corners.

XXV .ii

The false belief of touch. Love. That it lasts.
And always the blazing noon of the body.
Glint and cable-flash of sun on steel.
Black fleck dangled far above. Not suffering.
Not wisdom in death. Not dusk. But wonder.
The astonishing fiery wheel that carved each sky.
The faith that life had made a kind of sense
in making Bess' ripened years his own.
Faith in brine on the far side of streetcars
and the clear. That much. And then.
Their ragged descent, filth and slap of feathers,
hard bright things which would not shine but burn.

XXVI

Flesh: Not even his past held him.
          His skin a silvery thing unknown before,
          unchainable as water: never free
          but ever becoming so. He prophesied
          such harsh, luminous, here-of-the-flesh signs.
          The possible and the new. His lashed escapes
          offered hope to men soaked to the skin
          in alleys of trash. How is there hurt in that?

Latch: The lie that comforts is no less savage for it.
          He worked old forms: rust-bit fetters not his own,
          battered links, drab trunk-tricks bought at a bargain.
          Most himself when shut in dark cabs, railcars,
          or the granite hinge of lidded tradition –
          in the strange unmoored cast and drift of words
          flux and struggle held him fast; he knew all
          escapes are false escapes, that a work is roped
          to its past. Now men strut and mock him for it.
          They claim he lived too close to chains to find
          the dark hasped clench or lurch of a locked art,
          and drag back the bolt, and not be terrified.

Flesh: And there is sense in that. True freedom burns.
          Like cable, rope, cuffs, like electric light
          or aeroplanes he linked and forged the age,
          he learned his low opinion of mankind
          comparing men to chains.

The Circus
at the End
of the World

The poet awake and asleep – Welsh's Circus Sideshow – On the nature of the circus – Freaks – The Ring Lady – The Japanese Tumbler – Hatreds and ill omens – On illusion – Alchemy – The uncommon knot – The cat – Disaster and death – When the magnificence fades – Giftbearers – Prophecy and promise

XXVII

I re-entered the real startled and unsure.
A dark wind kiltered in, soaked the thin drapes.
White pages rippling. All bulge and roil and blur,

each poem was wrist or key and each escape
an incantation towards a darker chain;
I came to, as if here, in this house, to gape

out past glass at a world strangled by rain,
as a blacker surf crackles cold and white-crested
along a rock-strewn strand. I'd returned strange

to this coast, an apprentice poet posted
too long to his adopted flesh of chains,
lock-tackle, manacles, to any longer trust it;

to learn late Ehrich's large-knuckled shame
at work unfinished. The wet curtain stirred.
Shutting it fast I shut myself in again.

He who lived before me, in a lightless village, bundled fat in a rough-hewn crib while an old man trembled in darkness, mute, for I could not conceive the voice of a grandfather.

While in the sunlit yard: a filthy explosion of chickens at feed, the squealing of children.

And fate, its intoxicating scent like hot bread, fate tugging always at one's hem like a child's white hand, at what age did my father turn and bend to it?

I lived in debt to those who came before me, as anyone does, yet also looked to all who followed, knowing I must vanish without them.

And understood too late the frailty of my father's faith, long-buried, and the furnace of my own. The earth alone seemed admirable, the earth alone remained.

Stinking of sawdust, of sweat, I confessed to roped escapes which should not have existed, yet somehow did. Such feats men called miraculous, mistakenly so.

For miracles should exist and yet do not.

I admit haltingly, stumbling and confused, to events which happened long ago, to hunger and uncertainty in the circus trades.

Cold, blearied, we trudged past tents in a soft muckish field, old Welsh limping, fisting his lantern high: *Freaks keep back this way.*

I admit to rain cutting rake-like through our hides, to a bashed trunk dragging behind us in a wake of silt. And Bess, in her blown rags, weeping.

To helplessness, failure, the stink of horses in those lean years before the fame.

An elephant stooped, bronzed in mud.
Patient crate of wrinkles. All skin, flap of ear,
tiny eyes fixed sad on a puddle in trampled grass.
Watchful. As if to learn its earth well.
And in the wind a weary dog loped past, ribs tight
as coiled rope. A sack-cart tethered a black pony
to its shade. The air reeking manure,
reeling round a salve of heel-pocked pools.
Then out, beyond, big top, a broiling sky.
I swear all I witnessed there was real.

How favourably the circus of the past appeared in its day. Difficult
to imagine the seasonal virility of first ears of wheat, late rain in the air,
the electricity of cows heavy with calf, and yet necessary in order to
learn the circus as it was. High summer, flies in dead heat, main street
stirring with dust and sunlight only. Then: a hammering and a racket
pitched in a field empty the night before, sprouting just outside of
town as if by magic. A tremor beneath the streets. A muttering leaping
from porch to porch, gable to gable, like lightning. For in an era of
mud-filled ruts, bone-weary horses, of advance-men slipping into
town months early to paste gaudy banners along the walls of barns, the
circus became a creative act, it existed in the mind, more real each year,
bigger, ever more grand. The circus fed upon exaggeration, if the
eminent John Ringling is to be believed: two clowns became twenty,
any lady on a white horse grew at once hauntingly beautiful, stunted
elephants loomed ponderous as grain elevators. It has been observed
such institutions revelled in their strangeness. That pygmies, savages,
the miraculous Orient mingled with two-headed goats, fat ladies,
strong men lifting anvils chained to their eyelids. And all of this in an
act of controlled violence, of peanuts and crashing cymbals and the
always, always imminent fatality. Brutally trampled ringleaders,
plunging aerialists, tigers pouring fluidly from cages. Indeed the circus
seemed a marvellous invention in that century, before the more clever
methods of exhibiting death were discovered by our own.

— Consider slender Emma Thaller,
ossified as winter. Her face of sunken bone.
A warm flask of milk tucked in her bodice at tea.
Or armless Ollie, our human centipede.
Seventeen stubbed fingers dangling
from his ribs like feelers;
his toes ladling soup, shuffling cards.
How shy he seemed; secret as a key.

— The hinge clacked off the casements
all April, our trunk thudding stagewood,
its lid looming wide. I lay half-strangled,
hood-tangled again and again in rope,
getting it wrong, getting it wrong.
And Bess luminous in the footlamps,
Bess stepping forth as from a tomb.

— Suddenly eeling free of his shroud,
more moustache or eye-squint than flesh,
the photographer lurched,
flicked the plate,
snapped the catch and grinned.
Late sun glazed a wet guyline. Welsh scowled;
the clown lit a pipe; the aerialist twins snickered –
and the strong man slipped away in tights and dainty blue slippers.

— A ghostly clink of spoons,
a low dark breakfasting tent. The aerialist's omen:
that finch in the big top, its raftering wings.
Ari brooded, glowered, spitefully brooded.
Jim died a sloppy death, nothing more.
Brown crust of beans and yolk so like blood.
Far back in gloom, pale with unshaven grief,
the last aerialist ate alone
while in the yard a squall splattered mud.
All morning the mercury fell, it fell.

The sky terrified.

The curious Human Fly sinewed his ceiling to see.

Tall regret, without roof or ledge.

Squat stump of muscle,
stubby chandelier, he flexed, he leered down
his grotesque eyeballed leer, stirred the catholic air.
A mantel clock licked its palms, sang. He clung.
All things were falling always:
light rain, fragged brick, feathers. Bodies.
For the Human Fly'd not been outside in years;
he hung impossibly heavy and soft, in his mind
still clambering a skyscraper wall, muscular
and sneering, that bewildered window washer
peering from a birdstained ledge, a bucketed crate
of suds and rags soaping the tall air –
all of it wrong. From what did he climb, to what
did that man fall? A blackened earth spun;
the sky within the Fly's skull gaped.
He just
held on.

Arundhati Beejka, the Ring Lady of Babylon. Born into a century
reeling with salt-spars and rope-tackle, with thickening clouds of
industry, a century of empire, of science, of frail tempestuous painters.
The ocean was full, its shipping lanes teemed with spices, hundred-
handed gods, astonishing Oriental opulence. In other centuries she
might have lived out her life in the small fishing village of her birth, but
the peculiarities of fortune and horizon intervened and Ari, a peasant
girl of modest allure, enhanced by the exotic, awoke in the middle of
her life both well-travelled and well-read, a talented minor attraction
in the popular circus sideshow of the American midwest. Let us
summon the image with which she struck her contemporaries, as
recorded in the near-faithful diaries of James LBP Rotin, a respected if
staid physician of Hartford. First, the dim tent, the glint of dull brass
through incense and smoke. She would stretch languidly in the corner

upon a shabby cushion, almond-eyed, long-lashed, her skin more gold than dark. Still striking. A muscular diamond-backed serpent swaying like a tongue above her. Ari's laughter, if Rotin is to be believed, was smoky and coarse like the laughter of his late wife; he is careful to observe her generous crescent of belly, the quickening pulse of her more provincial customers. He notes her arms and legs were bound in heavy rings which were in truth a kind of almanac of her age, one for each year of her life. As if she wore the cold reassuring weight of time clinking against her flesh. She forgot nothing and recorded the events of each year without distortion. A perfect memory. Which was her true talent. And which meant a life without myth, without exaggeration, in a light always a little too harsh. The serpent and her copious flesh were of course necessary, for a long memory excited as little interest then as it does now. After all, nothing is less popular than the reminder of folly and of how little happens to the ordinary man.

Tetsuo Kudasai, the Japanese Tumbler. He taught the art of regurgitation, useful for any escapologist in the concealing of keys, training the esophagus and stomach to select from a number of swallowed items. For obvious reasons, lessons began with a small apple tied to a string. After the apple a brass ball, then two brass balls on separate strings, then no string at all. What drew Tetsuo east to America is still subject to speculation, for he understood little English, spoke even less, and few records of his passing remain. But we can ascertain a certain amount from receipts, artifacts, and gossip. In the one surviving photograph, taken on the 1898 Midwest Circuit, Tetsuo appears slender as a quill, withered, entirely hairless. He stands at the edge of the frame, dull white tights bunching at his knees, elbows, and waist. Of particular interest is his expression, for he is not looking at the camera but out, beyond it. Some have argued that his face appears clouded with melancholy, although the set of his jaw strikes contemporary experts as containing the strangled rage of men who have long lacked a collective voice. It is said Tetsuo was too old to perform at this time, and merely held the ladders and rope restraints for novice acrobats, which is likely, since the ill-fitting costume in the photograph is clearly not his own. Regardless, Tetsuo

was a man of dexterity and patience, acrobatic despite his age, as any
man must be who walks every day the tightrope of language in an alien
land.

The hard ugliness in holy men. All of us
God's billhook. Near old tarps nailed hastily
to ochre weeds I feared my father's shade
billowing in sunlight. Blue. As if alive.
As if the freak-circus frightened most
the mind. Thus the Fire-Swallower's death.
If the feral word burned, she told no one.
And our blind Albino's milky laughter
swelling her ribs. Translucent as jelly.
Silent, set apart, each in her cage of skin.
Ari weeping through her bars as I fumbled
at her lock bashed in by jeering boys.
White Ollie, stripped, laughed at, flogged
in a wet alley outside Providence.
The human strange made example of.
Be warned, you who avoid the savagery
of men. For skin indeed set men apart,
though it failed to make men different.
Mocked at, snarled at, shrieked and beaten back.
Born to it. But obdurate and ungiving.
All month we moved on, monsters bearing
tidings from an unimagined world.

Fiery blade-flints. Blood and invocation.
Sliced entrails splattering in omens.
The black arts. Lambs in that late season
of floods lay rag-twisted, limp, just meat;
ravens clustered in spells between rains;
farmers or mill-folk alike fled freaktarps
to wade instead the wind-shivering big top.
Flushed, flued, draggled, drenched in mud.
I was of that world: its seeping menace

mired wagons, bogged oxen, it bellied deep
our strangled horses, a plague of dark waters
long promised to us, as if to last our time.

The circus did not relent. Happiness meant frenzy, spectacle, crowd
devouring the self. But suffering also seeks embellishment. Thus the big
top fire. A blaze killing hundreds of farmers and townsfolk, its flames
almost intelligent. Fluid and arrogant, as if trained for the endeavour.
Later came the horror of steaming bodies, grinning remains of the
almost-human. But with it the extinguishing of chores, of belt-lashing
after supper, of hurt and lean wages and that particular cruelty granted
humankind. Fire as perfection and thus evidence of God. Though in such
language, as always, killing and horror are made myth. Which is the
agony of poetry and also its reason. For a crowd drawn to catastrophe is
more natural than one gathered in a drawing room after dinner,
catastrophe being a kind of radiance in the human memory. Terror, at the
close of an unhappy century. Stampedes and screaming. Black charneled
exits. Each forgetting in his panic that every yard of tarp lifts easily to the
blue roofless world beyond.

In another year, long since, when human flesh was not subject to such
welts, to the white juice and jaundice of ravaged skin, in a garden
without blemish.

When even I, who had thrived on hurt, sought the maple-lined path
leading to its gate.

For I had learned at an early age the limits of my talent and thus
discovered the nature of greatness, that there are everywhere gardens,
everywhere gates. Many are the gifted who fail because of their gifts.

Stubbornness was my strength. Though it could not lift barrels of
chains or bend iron girders, yet it bore the indignity of all who did not
see merit in the work.

Alchemists, scholars, rabbis, friends, all who toiled late into the night,
by lamp or bulb, to prove I was not in fact extraordinary.

How delicious, then, in the cold morning air, to feel my skin, my blood, and no longer listen to their words.

Stubbornness. Not the husked stubbornness in bark, but the hidden ache of muscle, bruise in the spleen, stubbornness of the dark anatomies.

So that I lived assured and strong in those years, ignorant of my fate.

Which, being brief, creaked heavily above the earth, above memory, distant hills, the lastingness in things. Which thus creaked importantly. Which shall not return.

It shall not return, it shall not return, it is, alas, no longer.

Among illusionists, the craft of illusion was not beautiful. The black arts were believed born from a fear of the human dead, and yet sorcerers illuminated the empirical earth more than most, as man's earliest poisoners, ancient surgeons, masters of metallurgy or the heavens. Recent French scholars have found merit in weighing magic alongside modern science, noting a shared faith in cause and effect. For in magic, as in physics, the gesture alters the world. Yet magic rites imposed strict and terrifying rules which, if neglected, incurred rope-drenched agonies, madness, worse. For this reason magical arts remained shrouded from men, as if maleficent or dreadful. The magician hunched furtively in his incantations, he chanted in guttural dialects. In the interests of scholarship, we must acknowledge the many theories of human deceit, deliberate and accidental, as if all ancient magic were false, in which case the sincere sorcerer braved far greater peril than the deliberate impostor. Yet to mistake magic for simple artifice is a further kind of deceit. For the illusionist abandoned his self to ritual, so long as it lasted. He believed the world must not be dismissed by physics, by the science of matter, but insisted instead upon wonder, the incomprehensible, the unknown. He faded quietly into irrelevance.

A sawdust art of thresholds, of what is taken from us, love, what is restored to us in time: magic, alchemy, conjuring, like shards of skull tagged in a cabinet.

Many the learned men, too frail for scroll or codex or leather-bound leaves, who deciphered its lean script in monasteries, beneath gates, on the banks of sluggish rivers.

Yet how guilty of folly its followers, seeking gold and untarnished skins; thus its rituals, light as quill bones, scraped dutifully in tall sunlit towers.

All my life, to tremble, exhilarated, in ice-locked harbours, knowing others had failed before me, sinking fast, hair seething in the earth's black tides.

Its victims cuffed, each to each, in an era of terror despite their struggles.

O my sweet flesh, forgive me, I knew well what punishments you
suffered yet lived no less greedily, lacerated and belted blood-tight.

As if to fast, meditate, abstain from desires of the flesh; for a time at
least, through ritual, to shed the adopted self. As if others spoke in me.

Understand, the old magic filled its shamans like a northern river,
braided, burning with cold, its gravel-lined bottom sure in waters
unseeable, in waters undrinkable and clear.

As in prayer, so in this art: wonder.

What we understand yet fail to comprehend.

I bent amid blooming mustard behind
the circus grounds to think again of him.
Rigid as a garden shovel. His strict heart.
I should have pitied it, his trunk grinning
in a kitchen corner, holy books leafed inside.
That ragged oak gold with sun beyond the glass
and him off stalking what he would be next.
No longer seeking ecstasy. Just time.
At the gate brown wagons baked drowsily.
Appleton all shadows, sinuous light.
Ma's long red Sabbath; her bending stoveside,
the smell of him there. That white sill where
she'd potted and watered his letters. He'd said
only in being sure of what we come from
are we capable of being other. In that place
I inherited the shabby faith of his wild
uprooted heart. His stiff-leathered trunk
less fine perhaps, but enviable, among forks
and knives and the old furniture.

Alchemy is the science of our folly.
Urging us to it. Pitch or soot fuming
in hot chambers of kilns, stoppers, casks.

As if distilled tin might be made pure.
As if in glass alembics an ash-like lead
burned to gold. John Dee, dreaded alchemist
and druggist, scried his spirits in a Stone
to learn the red blood of transmutation;
a singing lifted within him. Half-mad.
And the medieval Sicilian scholar-king
Frederick II locked slaves in a trunk to die.
To learn if a soul would seep from a gash
in a lid. The screams, scrabbling fingernails
like rats in wood. A terrible wet breathing
in the morning air. Thus do we desire
change and thus do we avoid it. Learning
what is around us we neglect what is
inside us, that vial of red mercury
we call the heart. A charred appendix.
The pale viscous poisons of the liver
or the lung's bellowed fire like flushed cinnabar.
Our minds made silver. Our minds white-gold.

Alchemy is only obscure because it is hidden.

He who does not understand should be silent or learn.

As above, so below; as within, so without.

The All is One, the One is All.

Wheat begets wheat, man begets man, gold begets gold.

Nature rejoices in Nature, Nature contains Nature, Nature overcomes Natu

Purify the five elements: earth, air, fire, water, space.

Harness the four humours: phlegm, choler, blood, melancholia.

Seek the stone of no stone, common treasure, the unknown known to all.

From dead stone, to be made living philosophical stone.

This, the Great Work, the glory of going on and still to be.

In Classical myth, the uncommon knot appeared rarely among men. As if untameable, it terrified. And yet with each appearance astonishing events occurred. First relearned while unbundling straw in a stable prior to Heracles' third labour. Later used in braiding the Minotaur's greasy hair. Loosed, it dragged plagues and great waves into port cities. Indeed, in the history of illusion, the uncommon knot deserves its own particular account. Herodotus describes it as musky, thick, like a muscled rope or python. Pausanius mentions its curious oven-like heat, its colouring as of bruised figs. In the Roman Empire's late years various emperors neglected duties of state in an effort to relearn its tying, the secret of which promised long life and fearsome worldly power. Yet during Rome's long decline, the uncommon knot vanished, hidden among mobs of unwashed human poor, as often happens in times of terror and barbarian learning. Apocryphal records do exist. In Lapland, wizards salvaged the art of tying wind, the looser the knot, the fiercer the storm. Medieval and Renaissance occultists such as Lull, Bruno, and Agrippa met often and conspiratorially with our subject. In 1705, local monks recorded the killing of an urchin for stealing charmed knots from a midwife; in 1798 the Bordeaux parliament burned an old woman alive for ruining a wealthy family with knotted cords. Thus the uncommon knot was gradually shunned, a dangerous companion. Old acquaintances blushed, lowered their eyes, crossed muddy streets as if on urgent errands. Memberships were revoked. Jobs inexplicably lost. Dark menacing fedoras loitered in doorways, at bus stops, engrossed in newspapers. In modern times the knot sleeps like a virus, fisted and hard, in the stomachs or, more often, in the throats of men. Clenching and unclenching. Struggling with its own body. From which we might, mistakenly, take comfort. For the modern man thus afflicted endures what would kill most men. He escapes, he survives, that is, he suffers longer than his fellows.

You dreaded clocks, Ehrich, hours, minutes, yet returned always to the vanished, the rain-eroded gravestone, the tree-lined avenue of childhood, as if origins obsessed you. I dreaded clocks, true, yet lived within origins, in an ancient shrouded trade, shamed, knowing how little survives beyond human memory. You speak of origins and the particular trade,

you who in truth merely feared being forgotten. I feared being forgotten,
confess it, though if weak I was no weaker than other men, and if while
honouring the graves of illusionists I suffered, tell me, does it matter that
sadness was my fate? A theatrical suffering, stacked backstage like a heavy
rug: that, and relentless memory, were your true talents. Yes, yes, my talent
Arbitrary, mortal, finite, frustrated, desirable because of its dying, your
celebrated life was in the end no different than his. No different, no.

Our cat slept his sinewy sleep of tail snips, of flickerings,
he dreamed of quarrelling crows:
with a slither, and a leap! in he'd go,
tearing feral amid their bickering.
All fang and tongue, a vast stretched yawn still not done;
all approached in stealth the mouth that ate itself.
For at dusk his shadowy twin
stretched daintily, stepped from him
and cat and shade came and went like smoke around the dinner tent;
old cat's a finer magician than I –
whisker-rubbed, panther-robed, sly
as molasses he'd sit on his barrel lid to wait and scheme and brood til day
When to the sun he'd turn a tolerant eye,
and yawn,
and sigh,
and solemnly permit it to rise.

Not the beast, but the feral intelligence
of darkness, midnight fanged and patient.
We hear its tread inside our skulls, it pads
along back alleys and clatters across roofs,
we fear witchcraft, the bestial familiar.
A raven scraping at the sill of our mind.
A furred black tail vanishing round the eye.
The hoofbeat beating bright muck and blood
back, back into us. We find menace
in the cautious fluidity of cats, agents
in black endeavours, like thinking shadows.
Always edging firesides, greedy lamps

swaggering in their eyes. Thus does it endure,
sleeping with fear tucked up over its head
til dawn. Like a blind man hiding his eyes.
Seeing no light but able still to feel it.
We'd walked in moonlight back of the big top,
Bess dark and sharp as a tarpknife, hair tangled
tight on her neck. To our pale sleeping tent.
When there before us hung a tail, hacked limbs,
a collar evil with fur. Bess's cat.
Strung in circus wire. Throated and swollen.
A gutted carcass, it grinned up, eyeless,
a slow-spinning sack of blood.

I cut the dead thing down.

The casting of evil spells is illicit and expressly prohibited and punished. This prohibition marks the formal distinction between magical and religious rites. We might go so far as to say there are evil spells which are evil only in so far as people fear them. In our tent Bess sickened, her skin turned a filthy ochre, sheet-stained, thin as wheat, her belly shrunken like sand. She drank little. Ari scrubbed a pale bulb above Bess's throat: *Ice her ankles, give salt – the dead fear salt.* I nodded. Her lovely reptilian eyes. Amber. Like a grin she was gone.

Survivor testimonies conflict, are vague, dark, as if torn out of the waist-deep wreckage. Welsh's train all at once lurched, groaning, to a halt. That much is clear. In the sleepers, lanterns crashed hard. Sheetbound bodies were hurled floorward. Men staggered up, out, into a shared darkness, luminous in white nightshirts and long-johns, fabric clinging to their wet skins. Rain, rain and the crazed white beams of lanterns drenching everything. The awful human cries of elephants along the rails. A trestle had splintered, hauling a railcar of horses down into the black waters. The menagerie lay crumpled, shred apart, its painted red-and-yellow sidings peeled clownishly back. Men milled fierce, waded half-naked into the flood to slash free frantic beasts, shouting angrily for rope, light, knives. Others dredged dead horses from the river. Heavy and frayed like rolled logs. A gunshot, then another, crackled up the gorge. Catastrophe, like human suffering, requires its chroniclers remain faithful to the facts. According to insurance files, what occurred on 16 September 1898 on the shadowy railroad through Virginia's Blue Ridge is best reduced to an act of God. And yet we must be cautious, as any struggle with an adversary of inhuman strength raises a quarrel with faith. True, our human talent is for order, shape, meaning. Therefore the fate of the Ring Lady, Arundhati Beejka, still perplexes us, even in light of later atrocities. An abomination precisely because it denies us sense. The terror of the inexplicable. Ari's railcar remained on the tracks, still lit, far from the horror. Swinging up, in the first to arrive, a feed man named Johnson, was astonished to find shelves of books intact along either wall. On the desk, her python slept in its crate, a rope of muscle, satisfied as stone. A sharp bite of spices in the air. Everything calm, ordinary. But Johnson is deliberate in his description of her body, its angle of repose, point of impact, the stain and spread of damage. Ari, it seems, lay in her bed, a mess of eyes, blood. Her wet brainpan exposed. A jagged shard of scantling driven through her head. While rain bloomed in through a small gash in the wall, while the brass coils on her arms glinted dully. The precision of the tragedy remarkable. Remarkable. As just at that moment, in a small fishing village in sunlight, an ancient woman no longer fully awake but frail now, fading, dreams of her vanished daughter. Beneath a crimson sky at dawn, the nets creaking below. Ari suddenly smiling, ascending the knoll up from the boats, slender as a drawn blade in the tall grasses, an old woman herself now, but youthful with memory, which is a kind of, yes, let this be the last word we write, kind of love.

Long October. White dust on the tents. End of all things.

In mulch grass a gold woman boulders lustreless, grim. Only her shadow moves.

Far east, ropes unfist. A bright tarp inhales, wrinkles heavily, falls.

The season shuts. Leavetaking. She leans, licks a nib, a blue charred nail.

Her paper crackles. Ink, black as grass at sunset. No wind.

In the mud sit three white pebbles. *They will be judged*, she writes, *those straights who shuffled on, solemn-thronged, grinning like the dead.*

The sun wades west in grass, speechless. Dry stone of light. *This too will be judged,*

she writes, *this hot sky wrung out, this hard earth filled with brass and bones.*

In the soil, white angels tremble, eyes raised at the many joyful feet

come to pass. Selah, selah, in an epoch of suffering and memory.

Alas, the skin as affliction, as a rash of water-blisters or boils; in my hands all flesh felt common and for this reason distasteful.

The hands alone weighed wetness, cold, the experience of air or sunlight against the imagined world, and learned pain, that ordinary condition of human life.

In this manner my exhilaration sickened, it failed slowly, like a long-held breath.

All summer, in glaring fields, sideshows swarmed with magic, illusions, the tired affordable repertoire I too lugged out, flowers blooming in a lapel, canaries vanishing, a clumsy second-sight act.

And all winter men in moth-eaten suits, unspectacular, dirty, filled dime museums with quaint card-tricks amid bootslush and freezing draughts.

Their real work finished, men more gifted than myself arrived at silence, the silence of age, the silence after that.

What had I to offer? Often I had stood bewildered, in blistered ropes at once loosed, my hands angry with secrets I was not let in on.

So that, trembling, fingering my skin, I began to doubt: had I accomplished this, who was not remarkable, no more than others?

This, which sang in me for a time, then fell silent.

Months of dust and rain, abandoned, in flickering railcars. It is true: to live without illusion is to live without hope.

Husked. Drained. Gutted. Until the burden at last was lifted, I had borne my share and now I too might laugh, seeing how foolish looked my staggering beneath it.

A kind of wastedness, my fists
strangling the pump, rusty waters
over-sluicing tin drinking pails.

Only menial ambitions in me.
Not asking awe of anything.
The splendour gone. Just craft left.
Failure and hurtfulness and hunger
in caravans, in cities of tents,
seeking the ways of strange tribes.
I was nothing, nothing, stubborn
with insignificance, bewildered
by an art's immensities
and blinded to all else.
Learning at last how it is
when the magnificence fades.

If guilty, then guilty of the possible.
Of legs eagerly chained. Of urging men
in struggle. Allowing awe which led
to myth, to rumours frozen fast
in Arctic ice. Buried hours without air
in coffins. In Madrid the garish signs
swore Nothing on Earth can Hold Houdini –
and yet the scent of Appleton's railways
in autumn after rain, *that* held; or Father
shivering in his coat on seething benches.
Devoured. Cheated. Mean. As if casually,
in guilt, I entered a savage century
treading once only its earth of trenches,
of human meat, the fallow soil filled
for future ploughs to drag up bent shrapnel,
sharp bones. Blessed, blessed, who stride it yet.

It happened. Bending, blowsy, in the lane
I felt it, a molten lead filling my legs
as Bess shuffled past dark firs, an old fence,
white-haired, frail, clutching a kind of parcel.
Below the garden, a slate ocean I did not know.
Suffering a dense blood to drag through me
its cold syrup. Surprised to raise gnarled hands,

liver-spotted, slack-skinned, and find a cane
taloned by one, yet afraid lest such surprise
fade from me, what it would mean. Thus we end
our days, thus all of age's thickenings
and easy humiliations go into age.
We drown in our bodies. All of it, somehow,
made fine. Bess trembling, all at once I knew
that parcel in her hands held words I'd waited
long for from one long silent. I reached out.
Birdsong, light, a warm wineskin and light.

Here, waking, I write in a faithful hand
all I'd witnessed that it might in time prove true.

In the circus at the end of the world
a book bound in hair held the names of human dead.

In the circus at the end of the world
dark angels dangled bat-like in the big top.

In the circus at the end of the world
ten thousand beasts, terrified, cried in human speech.

In the circus at the end of the world
weeping men barked and growled like bears.

In the circus at the end of the world
children fed on leavened bread and hands.

While buckets of meat soaked the crowds.
While the raucous long-trampled stones jeered on.
Beneath tarps shivering with laughter and malice.

In the circus at the end of the world.
In the circus at the end of the world.

A huge blue eye appeared, blinking.

A great hand reached out, as in wonder.

Music ceased. Frenzy ceased. All was shining
and calm, as it must be when mankind is no longer.

It seemed to us then a work fated to end
at last was ending. The human task no less
mortal than its age. Our earth's instrument
was time, which is loss, which is departure.
A crossing of open waters. A coach
loading at a black gate. Puzzled, perhaps,
by joy, as on a stool in a sun-drenched garden
an old man combs knots from his granddaughter's
hair. Her century already soaring

in the ropes of his. Alas, I thought
less through the flesh and more through the blood,
I could not comprehend this gift of escape
bestowed on me and no other, given
as if to transcend my station on this earth.
It is the year one thousand eight hundred
ninety-eight. All is ended. The pen lowers,
the book shuts, it shuts. Stillness.

To speak myself as another, to achieve a thing more stubborn than
the brief life. Posterity without shame, the bequest of a marvellous
thing well-made. Truth, if not fact. Talent, though not of the human
tongue. The unfashionable conviction that even misfortune makes a
kind of sense. The imagination as witness. A terse dense craft in
which the mouth must feel its way toward meaning. Compassion.
Attention. Praise. All I would work for in my time, this, serene,
luminous, holiest of keys, in the circus at the end of the world.

Book of Excision

His mother in sepia – The impenetrable heart – The seance – Visitors in the long ago –
The letter – An unexpected death – Grief and ghosts – Mediums and madness –
His attack on Spiritualism – Haunted by the real – The question –
Exhuming his father – Answers

XXVIII

Then, late, you longed to praise. To rake
weeping the wormed earth of her, and praise it.
Your naked wrists shining white and savage
in the cold cemetery dawn, fields smouldering
in the beyond. Grief. To praise the wet simple
stretching of the mind, your mother wading
her gardens at noon, the grey shape of her
hand ghosting a trellis, even the afterwards, you
damning her rhododendrons in the smoky July dusk
and meaning her. All of it. Death in her ribs
like a fire which fed on nothing and did not die.
The world does not know us by our hearts. Yes,
her heart, you sigh. Weighing the fist-sized bounty.
Amazed. Grieving importantly. Yet glad.
That untempered fire burning and burning
in the golden fields of your second life.

XXIX

Darkness. That parlour straked in dust.
A thick loam-heavy rug tacked at a pane
to muffle out the world. You sat afraid,
a child yet. Your mother coughed in her cuffs,
grief infecting her lungs. A gramophone
crackled out hymns in a mournful key,
its sinister brass throat glinting, the table-lamp
rickety and black-cowled. Then the seance began.
The medium's fingers dry and wispy,
his spectacles thin discs of light unseeable beyond.
His vision scorching. He shut his eyes –
Mayer, he groaned. *Mayer Samuel are you close?*
Your mother hunching in hard on her elbows,
that thick widowed thud of her heart gone big.
Then an eerie rustling of drapes. A softer dark
billowing in. And her sighing, eyes clenched.
A white teacup clattered its saucer; the card table
rapped like a knuckle, its legs bucked and reared,
your hands flat upon it felt it too; *Mayer* –
and all at once like feather or flack or furied
wing a thing battered past her chairback,
shrieking, all harsh gust and holy breath;
and a heavy blue smoke of burning lifted in you,
it lifted, left you animal-stunned and blind.

XXX

You listened shivering
at her bannister, one palm
flat on a thin peeling wall
purpling under your touch,
in the dark a darker sweetness
rising up like cut grass
etherized after rain,
her creaking attic door
creeping wide upon her and her
at a lit mirror writhing lithe
to clip a tangled thread
dangling down her spine,
her scissors rasping shut,
one elbow pinioned back
then bending birdlike out
and her graceful half-glowing
grimace grimacing in that glass;
or how she'd perch half-naked
upon a dragged-up chair
to mend some obscene knee-blown
stocking, its wrinkled hose
drooling across her thigh, sleeves
furrowed up in thought, her thin slip
tugged high, and her
thinking herself alone: slitting
the old seams, singing softly,
pressing one palm flat
on a battered table as if unaware
of that soft lumped whiteness
staring back at her, her flesh
lumped and creased by love,
since all marks of the flesh
become like marks of love –
and all of it spilling over, all of it
in the fullness of having been,
always, ever, taken in, and you
as if to yet be closer to it, listening

in a hall in the half-dark,
while that steady undiminishing
bell of light in her body
blazed out.

XXXI

All escapes died in you with her death. Theatres closed.
You wept before shackled trunks, uncomprehending.
The still harbour a grey eyelid salted shut.
While an armoured gangplank clanked in the dusk.
Its dark sailors weaving rail-locked, all throat, all bone.
A sun sank once, west, leering for that farther shore.
As if it, too, shrank from fog, ropes of salt rust, anchor chains.
Beyond landfall, crewmen dumped a man's trunk into the murky wash.
Shoes, sogged notes, trash slid like gulls in the swells.
What he would not need where you went.
The sky crouched in its cage of light –
all escapes died; you gripped a rail you could not leave:
few things opened where anguish did not follow.
Old stippled news clippings. Your father's sifting grave.
That telegram: *Ehrich she is stricken. Come.*
You were sick in those days, dreaming often.

XXXII

The rabbis believed illusion
the language of God. As if He spoke
in metaphor, dissembling. You mocked
their ancient miracles, minor arts
of escape –
                    yet gave in even to this
at her death, fixed to the cold stones
in Copenhagen among stampedes
of nostrils, chins, of suits pouring past,
Bess gripping your arm, that telegram
trampled bloodily underfoot
and a cello in an alley gutting itself
again and again into song.

Swarms of pollen
in the stung grass of Appleton.
A letter blood-brown with age
beside a bowl of shrivelled lemons.

Her table shines. A saucer
of milk on the stoop spoils
in the heat while a new brilliance
blazes its lip. It comes.
Comes in.

Sadness binds in glue and leather
her stitched letters left here,
it binds oil-light, light-etched envelopes
stamped in ink, the weight of her fist
impressing what once weighed on her,
on you. Worn. Well-thumbed.
Her plea for some reply
fading now, not yet faded
in your fist.

Then the black dream led to her.
The kitchen flickered, a muffled crash,
white drapes flung wide in a window:
her shade, like a lantern in scrubbed glass,
already shivering.

One of you is someone hiding.
A black sky in pustules of clouds, bursting.
Then rain, the frantic coughing rain.

It is said blood-oranges
weep when peeled. You punch a thumb
hard into husk, juice, sour meat of the rind,
the fruit does not mourn, splits seedful.
Her swollen lump-rouged skin
in its coffin, as dark fluids settled heavily in her,
as though even within her flesh, she wept.
And the darker juices fed nothing.
Healed no one.

The grain in her steel hair brilliant
at Machpelah with the white tombs
ablaze in autumn sun: to be blind
to the permanence of things, crustling grass,
fenders, frayed black threads, this long
funereal following. All your adult life
you lived without evidence of grace
to witness this one pure thing.

But shawled, laid out knit-black
in the parlour, enmeshed
and mild in a late casket
lately hidden. Death?
Widowhood cloaked her
black-buttoned, black-collared,
in the manner of stagehands
made all at once unseeable
and all the more wondrous
in being there and being
yet of use.

A gangplank rattled farewell. Oily swells, a lifting
hull, swarms of fat yellow gulls in foam,
a click as of a closed door –

So are you fed. The past is breadcrust,
the dead are draughts of wine, beloved:
what once was human in this earth
is ever human in this earth.

To the fragrant loam of Appleton
to the gravel or grit in rivers
to the earthy grain of boxwood
to mud to mire to clumped wet sand
to the smear of earth to the sludge of earth
to the meat of soil in the turned ground
to white clay shovelled from her grave
to the clay the white clay all are steadied
that in their turn might steady also.

So it is: what she is
no longer, this, being shut in,
her ruined garden in November under frost,
the sticky black rot in the pears,
is fading too. The evening of a season
blusters through Harlem.

Iron trellis, leaf-litter, rugged weeds
spurting along brick ravines,
her bleak ochre chimney gone cold.
This stillness has no centre.
The world forgets regardless.

Here where the ugly salt-shaker
squats upon her sun-drenched table
red drapes and dried roses lean
into incandescence, a dish of lemons
gleams dully, all is as it must have been
for her. The hour is late. Her scent
remains, a small room never returned to,
a footfall faltering someplace near.

Now a white sea has shut
between islands, a cloud of dark gulls storms in.
Dried lips, dried ankles: to have hated grief,
its stink of burnt things; now to ask a wetness,
to ask an oarlock's creak, old rigging, this tide
which fails to return, her touch which does not.

Lower the light,
the room bright
with a lit kindling
of men sweltering
in steerage, scared
in a smoky half-glare,
the black Atlantic Deep
ever near, like sleep;

then raise the light
as Bess' slight
tread squeaks and crawls
the carpeted hall
your mother's boxes fill,
untouched, still
in the hard relief
of a cramped encumbered grief
littering your landing every night.
O love there is one light and then that other light.

Unbuckling her closet trunk
to find water-foxed stacks of letters
in a hand not her husband's:
nothing is resurrected

but ever underfoot, in thimbles,
an old receipt, a luminous white thread.
Being in the world after her
was like staring at an ever shutting door
whose span of light kept shrinking
yet never wholly vanished.

You sip a smoky tea, thinking it.

But see, the filed ivory teeth
of her piano menace no one.
No keys to fumble now,
lacking her language of fingertips;
listen, this musty silence also
is song: a long rest,
then the held note of what comes next.

All this, bolted drizzle on sills, guttering rain,
this white soundless seepage, all this
slurs and drips the hinges,
her shutters gaping wide. Drag them shut.
Lash them fast. It comes.
The moon seeps like blood in the drapes,
its hurt stains them,
water-bearers, still-astonished hearts,
who for a time walked with you, walked with you.

Until at last, striding a dusky stage
it strikes you, their fear:
a rust of cuffs at your wrists, unlooseable,
the comprehensible terror of their lives.

For the real escape does not arrive.
Shared terror marks the common man,
a fellowship of death, failure, loneliness,
of men born only once to this earth.

Shared terror. All of them.
Which makes it, somehow, sweetly, bearable.

XXXIII

The only true freedom is clear conscience.
Though you had lived here once in brightness
and in joy believing otherwise. Alas.
The full hours go and come to.
Wisdom sinks from light to darkness like a stone in deep grass.
Such fields! Rustling with the shirr of heavy chains.
You ask the excellent language of the lost?
Sluggish ripple of sheaves. Black wind in the east.
That darker self dragging behind you through the wheat.

XXXIV

Shrouded lamps. Dour carpeting in parlours.
The blind spectre wavering incandescent
in a glass. Margery's gorgeous, Greek struggle
in her ropes. A Flemish medium fumbling
his slates in a dingy farmhouse outside Paris,
his mellifluous cursing at such clumsiness.
And old Alfred, dying in his shabby cot,
begging his legs be lashed together to keep
from falling apart. So much rope in all of them,
so much stubborn light to fool the heart.
You will forgive her, Bess said. There is time.
Locking hotel shutters as if locking in the light.
The dead do not return, not as you desire them:
in keys, perhaps, in keys pretending to be keys.
You longed for that life before her shrouding
when spirits still amused. Not yet haunted
by the real. When loss still seemed of use.

XXXV

The easy giving in of human reason
to the stubborn disregard we call the heart.
The way grief makes us eager in our greed.
Like mad Winchester's castle, its thousand locks.
And that stevedore strangling his infant son
at the urging of his dead wife's spirit.
His small bed squeaking later as he cried
to her. Or the blind chemist in her kitchen
late at night frying lentils laced in arsenic
to hasten to her beloved ghosts. In this manner
evil is made available to the heart.
Such madness is not faith. True faith comforts
no one, it confounds, is stubborn, it terrifies
in its immensity. No heart is huge enough.

XXXVI

The senses seem incomprehensible
to human reason. Men grope for hands
because. The startled heart slows and aches
so that. Bafflement at bedpans, kerosene,
a cold scalpel. Allowed a late wonder
lest little else console. The blind man cried
in that shabby hotel lounge in Kansas
while Bess bluffed her second-sight act.
Weeping in an imagined brilliance,
winter sunlight wending through the blinds.
As if his sorrow were a kind of seeing.
You suffered the flesh alone to touch and be
touched here on earth, intractable in its need.
And thrice after her death you hid in the den
and heard, at dusk, dark creaks in the porch
like rats or a racoon. Flung wide the door
to stand bare on a bare threshold, each time
comprehending, or almost. Like an aria
heard wharfside. Music so clear, the language
is made sense of. The two of you, in twilight,
shivering. A scrape as of feet receding.

XXXVII

       All month a plague of blackberries
in lumpen bowls, glistering wetly beside scripts,
towels, in buckets backstage – squinched billionfold,
eyeful, staring. The dead's blood-blistered widow-berry,
fat-backed spider-fruit, all ooze and split, its tart darkness
stained wrists, tongues, spattered bloodily down walls.
An evil sweetness filled those days, and nightly
the crowds thickened, a whir of soft sticky faces:
the purple teeth of mothers, the black teeth of mothers.

XXXVIII

How is it, in sealed trunks, I witnessed skies and starlight?

*The corners of the box which held you were never planking,
nails, smuggled keys. You were right to see as you did.*

And how is it I felt a bite of grass in that trunk, damp earth
beneath me? What were those heavy cries in the fields?

XXXIX

A squelch and slub of shovel-blade.
All day rain-bloated ditches made
digging difficult, floated spades,

foamed up flecks of rotted pine;
his sogged gravesite gushed a slime
of silt and peat and spill. In time

rain gattles all tombs: this grave,
bundled in tarps, gave and gave,
a gash you floundered in to stave

off flooding. Then a blade slit wood.
Clumped half-sunk in a soft hood
of coffin. Sifted its stew of mud,

flayed worms, seed-hard kerns of teeth.
All bilge and reek of meat and death.
Foul seepage. Like a long-held breath,

this, the harrowing of your father's
ribs and hair, a kind of brittle prayer
made bone of. To dig from there

those strags of him not led to God
and bury all back in holier ground –
a mud dense and thick as blood

in the murky rain. Mired in that pit
the hired man tightened, held his lips,
fumbled deep a dreeped casket grip

and groped beneath. You threaded him
a rope, winched it firm, that coffin
slucking noisily clear. Reeling in

and of a piece. Faith too is like that,
he'd believed: a thing hauled hard, set
to rights, a steady raising of the dead.

XL

Created capable of good and of evil.
Yet seemingly unable to distinguish.
So that small kindnesses inflict a kind of harm.
Not towards one, but away from another. This.
That she died. That now, limping and crooked, you want.
Alas, man selects his evil too often without coercion;
in truth you were not called; you might have lived many lives
absent with joy and fully of the world.
You chose this.

The Final Confidence
of Ehrich Weiss

XLI

And death arrived, as after a long journey, unbuckling its old sea-green trunk, smoothing its felted hatbrim, shrugging its coat upon a wall-peg drenched in the white sunlight of bay windows.

Or already leaked inside me, a dark syrup dreeping brackish in my flesh: the burst entangled ribbon of my appendix.

While a student in silver cufflinks flexed his fists backstage in Montreal, his blue eyes lowered.

Seven long days I lay veined in darkness like the grain in varnished oak.

As if holding to no illusions, here, at the edge of the inhabited ward, where wicker armchairs huddle miserably against a late afternoon glass.

To have shared in the recovery of an ancient work: enough for one life, perhaps. Alas that human memory is not more weak and pitiful.

As if here to utter a brief yes, a slight nod, nothing more, we who had forsworn the not-serious heart.

XLII

His grudging furrowed glare
as if the harbour in his eye
had already drowned him there,
that scuffled high bridge wide
with dark bowlers, grim stares,
and his sturdy sure-fixed strength
flexing at ease and at length;

and the stalled trams, the sleek
wedge-hulled barges in mist,
their anchored slurch and creak,
and the sagged glugged bits
of wet flyers in streets,
while in shop doorways men
peered out aproned and sullen;

the whole city held its breath:
market-stalls stilled, tall flags
slumped half-drawn as if death
had already dredged and tagged
his corpse, chains at his chest,
hard frown still biting back a laugh
as if all were but a photograph

or half-blown rumour overheard –
I'd smudged a sepia-stained date
in ink across one word:
1906. We learn wisdom late
if at all, our past is easily blurred;
I'd shackled myself to mine.
We drown in no element but time.

XLIII

White pears in jars floating fœtal and bald,
each glass glinting in our cellar, soft labels
dust-clouded on raw pine-shelves hewed up tall

behind the furnace. Through the upstairs door
long shadows savaged the light, shoved it thudding
deep-slatted step-by-step down. No stillness

ever seemed so still. I went into it often

after his death. For old Alfred in the end ascended
our attic stairs clutching hard
the dust-feckled railing, wheezing, as if not tethered
to the saved and sure;
knuckle-and-wrist first, hands mottled like old hide,
he'd clamber shakily up
to tag and stack water-foxed books from crates
snarled in a strawish stuff
or flaring his huge dewy nostrils like a draft horse
he'd huff and stamp
behind a shelf stippled with parchment rust,
all spectacles, cardigan, cough:
an old creaking of feet more floorboard than man,
more draught than breath.
Make it muscular and be apparent in it, he'd snort,
words are also escapes;
then stagger under stacks of letters, worm-eaten scripts,
catalogues, steel engravings,
sun-faded programmes, the filtered sift of centuries
staining his fingers like snuff.
Alfred slept in our garret in a tight book-clogged room,
his rickety bedframe
slouching wearily: a man come to wait out his age,
leafing through his life

as through a book, then shelving it snugly away,
a man of terrifying faith
who held himself before his God as others before a sculptor.
I think of him like that:
shuffling up our attic stairs, his stone-tufted scalp,
stone-tuberous ears
and half-eroded face flinching into sight, his eyes blank,
his stained teeth bared
as if in great effort, as from a great depth, his rising, up.

All his talk of inheritance and what was due.
We inherit parentage in what past we choose

to live from; and year on year are fathered often.
I found in him a father and found my father in him,

a throat believing evil inevitable as breathing,
that faces soft with age will harden before death.

Alfred, fine pen. I left your famed French sorcerers
early, loathed Robert-Houdin – that lousy magician and liar –

for each occult tradition earned and entered into
once entered into its own bloodline. This we elect too.

In Arles I shut sadly your *Art of Collected Sleep*.
Such old luminous works of magic seemed eminently

sensible: we do not come from who we are,
ever parting from it, do not seek our part

in a wholeness so full it overspills the guts;
our inheritance is not awe and never

love. Not that. His attic brooded with rats,
dark lamps sinister as dead clocks, brick sills
and shelves gutted without sun. *Mr Houdini*,
he'd mutter, *we live obligated to this time too.*
I'd lean in; he'd sift leaflets, playbills, books,
coughing a clotted brown yolk from his lungs,
rubbing a burnished wrist, its tiny coat hanger bones.
One cold afternoon in his illness he stiffened,
peered at me. Through the heating vent Bess' voice.
Singing an old carol. And he wept. In the half-light
open books were the pale cupped palms of children,
his cough a brittle rasp of trunk, an old scent,
whiteness.

I went into it often after his death,
the shades of pale tins, mustard hooks, raw lumber
looming in the cellar murk; and sat sock-footed

on the stairs, dredged up, dragged sleepless out
and set brooding down, far from our attic. In my fists
his locked diary shut fast, shining. A polished mirror

startled by its own cold brightening stare.

XLIV .i

The photographs. Wet mutilated heads
of Chinese raiders seeping cabbage-like
in a ditch, bodies dumped in river-weeds.
A girl's gouged-out breasts, her grisly tight

agonized grin as blades gored her. Filling
late hours alone leafing old books to stare
into the fleshly fine-edged craft of killing –
fiery pain in the likeness of prayer –

and see in the blue light at last beyond it.
What was my father's God if not of this?
Engravings, too, of gibbet-strung tortured
Jews, of witches carved into confessing;

like anyone, I lived oblivious, believing still
in dreams: evil too seemed a kind of truth
ever coming true; there was no finished evil.
We had only faith to harden us here on earth.

XLIV .ii

Then the bound no more believed in blood or chains
or aged books; escape grew commonplace;
the thin insane ropes no longer kept men sane.

Magic was tagged and filed and in time tamed
by ethnographic texts: a safer kind of grace.
The bound no more believed in blood or chains.

Fierce rituals, fierce thresholds, fiercer shames.
Death felt distasteful to all, a casual disgrace.
The thin insane ropes no longer kept men sane

and the dark face once feared, science now explained
with mirrors, with light; the arts of reflection were lost;
the bound no more believed in blood or chains –

and all were bound. A kind of inattention
passed as hope. The great writings rotted unused.
The thin insane ropes no longer kept men sane.

No knot is inescapable, men grinned. *All change
can be stepped out of.* Such grim bright lies.
The bound no more believed in blood or chains.
The thin insane ropes no longer kept men sane.

XLIV .iii

In the dream of endless incantation
the brownstone curled in fog I rapped upon
and listened at felt stilted and familiar.

Both mine and not mine. Then its gate creaked in
and I saw no lock or hinge but there I was inside
a dark academy of conjurors

unable to awake. Fixed bolt-heeled and hard
below stern frowns of the great marbled dead.
Men I'd known. My face too glared blindly down.

Windows. A deep gloom. A shirr of thick drapes.
Then the drawn intent silence of a hushed crowd
I swear was real and with me as I slept.

XLIV .iv

> Not escape. Release.
The old locks struggled *with* me, creaked wide
eagerly the way books once opened for my father;

rubbing the white gash and gouge of wrist-flesh
I'd think of it, a glared light behind his door
as if his soft reeking candles shone yet

over that bloodoak cabinet he'd studied at,
hunched thin, his thumbs marking line by line
his prayers. It was never about escape;

in both of us the tine, prick, snag of keys
lodged in hard flesh rustled at our sleeves:
sore buried things carried in us all our days.

What did it mean to be tied? Imagine
a fist of light in your flesh, imagine it
opening: a finger of rope had frayed

in me, I feared its unravelling darkness.
As if the binding held some meaning.
Escape flared in the sinewed knot itself

and needed only to be trusted to,
a kind of craft of unquestioning;
the true release is all loop and slow coil,

it draws ever tighter. Nightly in the walls
I'd hear rats fall like slaps of rope; then stillness;
then only the dark hall-clock unwinding.

Swivel-and-snick splutter of a turned handle.
Bald knob bare in the palm. The torpid click
and calm take of springs triggered far within.

I'd set myself to hear it clear again,
that ordinary hinge and creak and drag
of doors we live with all our days and lose

the wonder of. That scraped, trued, tug and heft
of hands. Sullen give of the wall I was.
And in my fifty-third year I found myself

still capable of astonishment, only to be
made more so: set to the dark art of doorways
I learned instead the art of stepping through.

XLV

It is true, I was thrust into blood-greased hands at dusk; and named
Ehrich; and tied fast, warm as a thumb.

And it is true, draped in stiff sheets, in hospital, in 1926, I died Harry
Houdini. Stomach stapled shut. Blood-greased, grinning, on Halloween.

Thus I failed two lives, although it will be said, like anyone, I failed others.

In the years between those lives, a tousled child gripped his mother's
skirts, feverish, unable to sleep, while fields flexed and groaned in rain.

And in the green hedges of Appleton, sun-browned, solemn, two brothers
hunted squirrels with armoured pinecones, listening for their father's
crisp staff.

But now when I return: bricks, sunlight striking glassed storefronts,
alleys, asphalt, nothing is as it was and my recollections begin to fail.

To only amuse, or to stir a world? I did not set myself this task and,
abandoned, remained blind to it.

While others used wisely what was given to their keeping here on earth.

And yet, to notice so little in the brief time given us, that in the end we
are astonished even by common rope.

In Appleton I'd glanced once and there a black ox stooped, bouldering,
in a bronze field. And glanced again and found only tall grass, shirring.

Not regret, exactly. But between the two glances: a lifetime.

XLVI

Backstage lamps coaled a soft red; lead pipes
ticked in the cold; a door clicked shut. I shaved,
thin knots of blood at my throat, the skin white
like Father's spaded bones hauled up in rain –
teeth pale in the grass, a sky tilting, thunder
ascending the blustering dark slope toward us.
That had been all. An icy rain drizzling
slow into my collar, red cheeks wind-stung.
The blade rasped, splashed quietly in the basin:
dulled razor, stained mirror, crumpled towel,
thirty years glaring hard at me. His face bared
piece by shimmering piece; he never really died.
Each day began a disappointed face in the glass
and ended a disappointed face in the glass.

XLVII .i

I lay still breathless. That leather sofa
sagged and creaked backstage in Montreal,
it peeled stickily from my spine. The drag

of heat in the halls, the scrape of charcoal
a student sketched and shaped my likeness by,
my face like a lock rusted shut by age;

I lay breathless, still remembering
the cold give of nails sinking into wood
onstage, the stink of camphor, a silence

lightening the weight of what-came-next
while that pale student scratched in his pad
this last kind of mirror I'd appear in.

I'd once thought virtue a vital thing
as fleshily of us as a ruptured lung
or a black devouring cut from our throats,

I had thought us accountable for all
that outlasts us. I cocked an elbow sharp,
lifted my aching ribs from the leather

and glancing at the door's looking-glass saw
a likeness lift thick and ugly as an old root;
it was not mine; a double of the mind's eye –

and, heavy-lidded, tight-lipped like a box
I alone had peered into, that darker thick-set
reflection spoke: *Is it true, sir, you claim*

to withstand any blow to the abdomen?
The fat yellow bulbs, the fiery sheen
of the costume-trace. A dazzled shock of glass.

Such splendid brightness juddering
against the cold deep terrifying sureness
in his hands: had I known him even then?

Fists flexing whole because holding nothing
but bound light, he strode from the mirror
diaphanous, drawn down like a shade,

to hurl, startled, each impacted punch
in fact set to strike long years before
but landing on me viciously just then –

God's phenomenal burst and flare of heat
rupturing my side, that gasped ripple of grief,
that travelling-the-flesh-of-it all up out of me.

XLVII .ii

And when his muffled fist hit, bold right hook like a bolt
of hide-breached hang-laced leather, I whirled unstitched,
                dressing-gown hurled hard with it
where I slumped crumpled shirled, clownish and loose as a colt;

when, dressing-room pitching lamped above, as the fine slack
recoil struck in me an elastic snap and buckle of ribs,
as my body sank, sucked into itself, back, in, old

with suffering I gulped and flailed, a being of bloodlet, burled
in bone
            I leaned full flat, I lugged a leg across the world

and in falling felt the fierce indifferent bash all flesh is.

XLVIII

Strange to lie so still.
As if my hands dreeped
riddled in grey mud.
As if already earth.

Or the soft puddle
of Bess' clasped palms
curled in mine.
Flesh I'd lost the feel of.

Each ochre nail
weeping from its finger.
Each lug of thumb
cocked listening.

A full slubbed
silence pooling
like fluid in the joints.
Her hands raised

rigid and grudging
in the mind's eye,
their dark meat
devouring all they'd held –

love, in the grip
of a long grieving,
lest all she'd touched
be in the end untouched.

XLIX

The final confidence of Ehrich Weiss.
An iridescent shine flooded
the hospital from within. Lamps. Halls. White beds.
Against stiff-cushioned seats Bess slumbered.
His hand held mine in a rumpled shrug of sheets.
Calloused. Less mine to take than be given.
Yet it was given. And it was taken.
For in a kind of lightening of breath he'd left Bess briefly.
Paused as if unsure at the wedged door.
Its threshold reeking of rivermud in Appleton,
of lush weeds rotting in black water.
Then his ruddy raw-boned fingers led me from the ward.
Huge clocks silvered, like storm windows. The light died.
All felt hushed. A stillness not of absence but of fixed attention.
A stairwell we'd slung a leg wide and slipped clear of.
I understood then a thing had finished.
And all at once, ablaze, a door burst wide in a wall
and he stepped out through. A light-drenched, lockless door.
And I saw he had been bound all this time:
elbows pinioned to his ribs, skin rugged with sores.
The black ropes reluctant. Tight-veined. Old.
Forgive me, Ehrich, that I stood, even then, astonished.

Above the black river
loomed black girders long barnacled
by a cold wind-riddled rust; high upon it a black crate
gaped wide like his blood-chambered heart.
I stood alone before what lay within it.

Reeling in oily woodsmoke.
The river's black bolt of cloth just beyond the moonlight;
a river beyond the river.

Is it possible to regret so little?
Bent elbow to ankle in cold chains

while old currents rigged their whitened hands
toward that crate, that tackled crate
close to love. And yet –
my skin, too, hurt once, was real.

Dying is dreaming such hands, a key in such hands.

All this in joy. The bite of onion in salt.
Dark earthy gusts of rain. Hearing again
in a train station his fierce gritty shout.
Or Bess lathered, ill-lit, in a claw-foot tub.
Shining faucets. Theo's husky thick talk
of boxing. Lesser things: the snikt of a latch,
wheeoo of a radio, spit of fried grease, all of it,
the rich heavy musk of Appleton in harvest:
how fine, having lived among them.
It had seemed only a moment, this life.

L

Of course it was a metaphor. All coffins are.
In sunken light the tank – a pool lustrous
all morning – sloshed glinting a bright water;
then that glass-lidded casket steadied in it.
He lay full-lit in a streaming dawn light
staring up through glass-shine, water-shine, up
into the clear attentive shade Bess cast.
And calmed. His thighs stuckled slimy walls.
His shaking fingers stilled. The coffin lid
bleared, runnelling sweat; gasping, slurred
as if drunk, he stretched thin as a sheet, bones bent
all-angled, the taste of keys pricking his tongue.
A dripping incandescent heat like a lamp
blazed on. No escape. Submerged an hour.
What is it in water that illumines?
He felt light-headed, brilliant, breathing full
with sweet fortune; and staring up at Bess
staring in at him it seemed all men live
drenched in the same light: what is best in us
refracts in us. It was a trick any might learn.
Just lie very still. Shut your eyes.
Exhale.

LI

Then the world's ropes untied themselves and it was understood how much men relied on being bound. Ships unmoored; crates fell open; the tongues of shoes gloped sloppily out; even scarves, being a kind of rope, slid mournfully from coathooks and hangers. And the only sound was a soft dull sump like wet snow sliding from a roof. Everywhere the relaxing of ropes forced a tensing of muscles. As if to remind what is not borne by one is borne by another. And all of it quick as a sigh, before the knots flexed back, before the reptile stillness of the ropes resumed. But in that moment something had been loosened. Men who did not smoke fumbled for cigarettes. Secretaries stared mournfully at dark typewriters. Schoolchildren waded through luminous gold rivers of leaves, listening. Thus does the marvellous interrupt our lives. Brief, and particular, and unseen. But there among us. Another kind of grace.

LII

Bridges, flashbulbs and rain: in dark rivers
I grow lean, grey. Sadness; is it this?

Rib bones fatten like trout against the lungs.
A breath, and they lazily ripple in flesh.

We thicken, grow sluggish on strange bread, faith
that isn't faith: black burst appendix; desire

gone bad. In the waves a tiny sun swims, leaps out.
That sudden bright distance between us.

Harry Houdini: Biographical Note

Ehrich Weiss (1874-1926) lived his early years amid the squalor and notorious slums of Milwaukee and New York City. His father, Mayer Samuel, had failed to find employment as a rabbi in his native Hungary, and in 1876 emigrated to Appleton, Wisconsin. Two years later, by steamship, his wife Cecilia, and their children, including Ehrich, joined him. America should have marked a hopeful beginning. Instead, here began a period of poverty, failure and upheaval, as Samuel, who did not speak English, lost job after job and found himself without appropriate skills in a fiercely-competitive immigrant world. By the end of his life, ashamed, he was working alongside his young son in a sewing factory in New York. He died of tongue cancer after Ehrich turned eighteen. On his deathbed he begged Ehrich to look after Cecilia.

Ehrich had been fascinated by a touring circus while in Appleton, and years later his interest in magic was rekindled by the autobiography of the infamous French conjuror Robert-Houdin. Taking this name as his own, the adolescent Ehrich called himself Houdini and set about learning the art of magic.

But Ehrich was a mediocre magician. He could not afford to purchase the better tricks, and found himself performing hackneyed flower-in-the-lapel gags to mostly empty vaudeville houses. He toured for some time with the Welsh Brothers Circus, where he acquired skills he would later adapt for his escapes: regurgitation, flexibility, dexterous toes. During this time, he met Beatrice Rahner. Two weeks later they were married. He was nineteen, she was eighteen.

With Bess assisting him onstage, Ehrich began to specialize in a minor – but startling – aspect of his performance: handcuff escapes. He very quickly rose to headliner status. His success was owing in large part to his innovative handling of the press and to promotional events before a week's performance, like escapes from straitjackets while suspended over busy city streets, or manacled leaps from bridges to escape underwater.

Ehrich toured England, and then Europe, and everywhere met with the same success. He was most popular in the repressive regimes of

Germany and Russia. Fascinated by modern technology, he purchased an early Voisin aeroplane while in France and had it transported to Australia. He was the first man to fly on that continent. By this time Houdini was one of the most famous men in the Western world.

In 1913, while still in Europe, Ehrich received word of his mother's collapse. He sailed at once, but did not arrive in New York in time for the burial. Cecilia was laid to rest in the Weiss family tomb, beside her husband (whom Ehrich had exhumed and moved there some years before). Ehrich never recovered from the loss. In his grief, he consulted Spiritualist mediums, who claimed to contact the dead through "spirit guides" by levitating tables, producing ectoplasmic shapes, and conjuring shadowy figures. When Ehrich realized that these mediums were using the tricks of the escape-artist to dupe their clients, he set out to expose them.

Houdini turned more and more in his later years to scholarly pursuits. He established one of the world's largest private libraries on the history of magic, laid out plans for an academy of magicians, lectured, and wrote a number of books denouncing Spiritualism.

In Montreal on his final tour, a student backstage challenged his claim to be able to withstand any blow to the stomach. The student punched him three times in quick succession before he'd had time to prepare himself. Two days later he was rushed to hospital with abdominal pains. He died on 31 October 1926 from complications of a burst appendix. He was fifty-two.

Notes and Acknowledgements

Earlier versions of these poems have appeared in the following journals and anthologies: *Breathing Fire 2* (Nightwood Editions), *Grain, Canadian Literature, Fiddlehead, forgetmagazine,* and *Prism International.* I am grateful to the editors for their support.

✤

While I have not hesitated to alter facts where necessary, I am indebted to the following texts for their historical and biographical accuracy:

Kenneth Silverman, *Houdini!!!* (HarperCollins, 1997).
Ruth Brandon, *The Life and Many Deaths of Harry Houdini* (Kodansha America, 1995).

In poem XXVII, the list of alchemical principles is adapted from Peter Marshall's *The Philosopher's Stone* (MacMillan, 2002). "*The casting of evil spells...*" is quoted from Marcel Mauss' *A General Theory of Magic* (Routledge, 1902).

✤

I would like to thank the following:

Jacqueline Baker, Erika Baxter, and Jeff Mireau; Lorna Crozier, Charles Wright, and Rita Dove; Patrick Lane for his wisdom and guidance; the UVic and UVa Writing programs; my editor Stan Dragland, and the staff at Brick; my family for their support, especially Kevin Potato; and, above all, Esi Edugyan, for her faith and fiery mind. She is, quite simply, my Bess. Heartfelt thanks.

Steven Price was born and raised in Colwood, BC. His work has previously appeared in literary journals in Canada and the US and a selection of his poems appeared in the anthology *Breathing Fire 2*. He has degrees from the University of Victoria and the University of Virginia. He currently teaches poetry at the University of Victoria.